Medieval Ornamental Styles

THIRTY-SIX PLATES IN COLOURS

WITH GENERAL INTRODUCTION AND DESCRIPTIVE LETTERPRESS.

BY

W. & G. AUDSLEY,

FELLOWS OF THE ROYAL INSTITUTE OF BRITISH ARCHITECTS,

AND AUTHORS OF SEVERAL WORKS ON ART.

CHARTWELL BOOKS, INC.
A Division of
BOOK SALES, INC.
110 Enterprise Avenue
Secaucus, New Jersey 07094

First published in 1882 *as Polychromatic Decoration*
This edition first published in the United States in 1988 by
Chartwell Books Inc.
A division of Book Sales Inc.
110 Enterprise Avenue
Secaucas, New Jersey 07094

Produced by Brian Trodd Publishing House Ltd
London, England

ISBN 1-5521-337-5

Printed in Italy
by Tipolitografia G. CANALE & C. S.p.A. - Turin

CONTENTS.

TEXT.

PLATES WITH EXPLANATORY DESCRIPTION.

CONTENTS.

PREFACE.

It is a somewhat remarkable fact that, amongst the numerous works which have of late years issued from the press, not one has professed to be a systematic Treatise devoted to the Polychromatic Decoration of Ecclesiastical and Domestic Buildings in the mediæval styles. Books have certainly been published which contain fragmentary illustrations of mediæval ornamentation, and some others have appeared in foreign countries, devoted to the monographical representation of the polychromatic decoration of modern or restored ancient buildings. Valuable as such books are, they scarcely meet the demands of the present time, in which a practical and suggestive guide is much wanted by all who have anything to do with this branch of decorative art.

Such a want the present Work attempts in some degree to supply; and although it is not intended for those who are already skilled and learned in the subject, yet to them it may occasionally prove useful, by supplying hints. To students and younger members of the architectural profession, to decorative artists, and practical painters generally, it will form a valuable and suggestive book of reference, containing designs based upon ancient authorities for the characteristic ornamentation of the various portions of ecclesiastical and domestic buildings erected in the several styles of Gothic architecture.

To those amateurs who amuse themselves by decorating their own dwellings, furniture, etc., or who lend practical help in beautifying their village or country churches, this Work will be of great benefit, for it contains more hints and suggestive designs, systemised for their use, than can be found in all the works already published on the polychromatic decoration of mediæval buildings.

The Plates are most carefully and accurately drawn, and as great a variety of features introduced as is possible in each one; while the accompanying letterpress describes the use and various artistic combinations of the designs; and supplies hints for their adoption and arrangement on the walls and other parts of buildings.

W. & G. AUDSLEY.

Liverpool, October, 1881.

POLYCHROMATIC DECORATION

AS APPLIED TO BUILDINGS

IN THE

MEDIÆVAL STYLES.

INTRODUCTION.

It is now an acknowledged fact that in all the great periods or styles of architecture, painting was freely resorted to for the purpose of accentuating the ornamental details, and embellishing the walls and roofs of buildings. The Egyptians and Assyrians painted their temples, habitations, and tombs : and the Greeks and Etruscans were thoroughly versed in all matters relating to the coloured decoration of buildings; painting was recognised by them as the great handmaid of architecture.

The system of colouring and the method of its application to the various architectural features are well known, so far as Egyptian art is concerned; but of the exact modes resorted to by the Greeks, which have long formed a fertile subject of speculative discussion amongst architects and others, we have comparatively little information. As polychromatic decoration in relation to architecture generally is not the subject of the present treatise, it is quite unnecessary for us to enter upon the consideration of the several methods of painting as applied to the great works of antiquity.

The barbarous nations of northern and western Europe were not behind the southern and eastern civilisations in the lavish use of colour in their architecture. That they showed less refinement and a greater love for the primary colours and gilding is highly probable; a rude and fantastic splendour would be better appreciated by them than the quiet richness and refinement which obtained in the arts of Egypt and Greece.

The Romans were probably the first who weakened the union between painting and architecture; erecting temples of marble and stone without applying colour to the surface of those materials. They could not, however, discard the painter's art altogether; finding painted decorations highly effective on flat surfaces, they freely applied them to such walls and ceilings as were finished in plaster. The architecture of Pompeii and Herculanum was painted internally, and in many cases externally, with the greatest richness. Colour was carried over all

A

columns, entablatures, walls, and ceilings; the floors sustaining the general effect by being covered with mosaics of coloured marbles.

Leaving Pagan times, and turning our attention to Christian art, we still find an intimate union between architecture and painting; and we can trace this union throughout the whole of the important works of the middle ages. There is little doubt that painting was resorted to with the object of adding richness and uniformity of effect to those portions of the earliest Byzantine churches which were not constructed of precious marbles or covered with still more precious mosaics. It was to Byzantine art, indeed, that, for several centuries, the artists, and especially the painters, of the west looked for their inspiration.

All researches made in the styles of Christian architecture, commonly known under the general term Romanesque, tend to prove that the early architects designed the interiors of their buildings with the view to their ultimate completion by painting, and that surfaces were purposely left for its display in preference to the adoption of sculptured ornament. The details of Romanesque architecture cannot fail to strike the observant student as being peculiarly adapted to receive painted enrichment; and the mouldings, the massive cylindrical pillars and the simple cushion-shaped capitals seem to call for accentuation and relief by a system of polychromatic decoration. That all these architectural features were painted with appropriate patterns we have ample proof; but unfortunately enough original work has not been preserved to our time to enable us to form a clear idea of the systems of painting followed by the Romanesque artists. The perishable nature of mural painting, in the cold and damp climate of the north west of Europe, has rendered it a hopeless task for the student to look for more than the faintest indications or the most fragmentary remains of work of early date. The Romanesque artists doubtless derived much inspiration from ancient Roman and later Byzantine works; and it is to the still existing remains of the latter school of decoration that we must look for a clue to the styles of painting adopted by the early Christian artists on this side of the Alps.

The mosaics of such churches as St. Vitale, SS. Nazareo e Celso, and St. Giovanni in Fonte, at Ravenna; the cathedral of St. Mark, at Venice; and the twelfth century cathedral of Monreale, near Palermo, supply much information; but we find more in the careful examination and comparison of Byzantine and other manuscripts executed in the west prior to the thirteenth century. It is beyond doubt that the ornaments of manuscripts would largely partake of the character of the architectural paintings which obtained at the period of their execution, allowance being made for the individual fancy and invention of the illuminator, and the license his art allowed him for their free indulgence.

We do not wish it to be understood that we incline to the belief that the artists of western Europe ever thoroughly appreciated the rich and glittering magnificence of Byzantine decoration which spread itself over walls, arches, and vaults without any apparent desire to accentuate or develop the lines and structural divisions of the architecture. To the mediæval artist of western Europe, architecture chiefly existed in its rich lines, pleasing combinations of form, and relief details; by all of which effective results of light and shade were produced : and in the application of coloured decoration all these lines and forms had to be recognised and left undisturbed. In this respect, at least, there is little doubt that the Gothic decorators followed in the footsteps of the ancient Greeks.

Mr. Viollet-le-Duc justly remarks (1) : " Painting as applied to architecture can proceed in two ways only : it is either subjected to the lines and forms of the structure; or it is quite independent, extending freely over the walls, vaults, pillars, and mouldings.

" In the first place it is an essential part of architecture; in the second it becomes, so to speak, a decorative furniture, which has its own peculiar laws and often destroys the architectonic effect, substituting an effect belonging exclusively to the painter's art. That painters consider this last kind of decoration the only good one is hardly to be wondered at, but whether art gains by it is a question well worthy of being discussed. Painting was separated from architecture only at a very recent period, namely, at the Renaissance. When the picture, the isolated painting, made in the artist's studio, took the place of painting executed on the wall intended to preserve it, architectural decorative painting was lost. The architect and the painter worked each in his own direction, deepening every day more and more the abyss which separated them, and when by chance they tried to unite on the same ground, they found they no longer understood each other; and desiring to act in concert, there existed no bond which would unite them. The painter accused the architect of not having left him suitable spaces; and the architect considered he was right in declaring that the painter did not take into account his architectural dispositions. The wide separation of what were formerly two brother arts is felt when we cast our eyes on the attempts made in our day to reunite them. It is obvious in these attempts that the architect has neither conceived nor realised the effect which painting was to produce on the surfaces he prepared; and that the painter considered those surfaces simply as pieces of canvas stretched in a studio less convenient than his own, never troubling himself with what would surround his picture. This is not the way in which decorative painting was understood during the Middle Ages, nor even during the Renaissance; and Michael Angelo, when he painted the ceiling of the Sistine chapel, did not isolate himself; he was thoroughly conscious of the spot and the place where he was working, and the entire effect he wished to produce.

" The fact of a painting being upon a wall instead of a canvas does not necessarily make it monumental; and almost all the mural paintings produced nowadays are nothing but pictures, despite the difference of procedure in their execution; therefore, we see that these paintings demand framing, that they group themselves into scenes, each having a point of view and proper perspective, or that they develop themselves into processions between two horizontal lines. It was not in that way the ancient masters in mosaic or the western painters of the Middle Ages proceeded to work. As to decorative painting, hazard, instinct, and imitation alone serve as our guides at the present time; and nine times out of ten it would be difficult to say why such an ornament takes one form rather than another — why it is red and not blue. One has what is called taste, and that suffices, it is believed, to decorate with illumination the interior of a structure; or else one gathers from different quarters fragments of paintings to apply them

(1) *Dictionnaire Raisonné de l'Architecture Française.* Vol. vii, page 57.

indifferently — this one, which belonged to a column, on a plain surface ; the other, which was on a tympanum, to a base plinth.

" The public, frightened by these bedaubings, does not find the effect very good ; but it is proved that the decorations of the Middle Ages have been carefully consulted, and that same public accordingly concludes that the decorators of the Middle Ages were barbarians, which is, by the by, very willingly granted.

" In the decoration of architecture we must confess that painting is perhaps the most difficult part, and that which demands the most careful calculation and the greatest experience. During the Middle Ages the interiors of all buildings, the richest as well as the poorest, were painted The artists had certain data, defined rules, which were followed by tradition, and accordingly the humblest of them could not go astray. But now these traditional rules are lost, and each artist is free to seek out laws for himself : we must not, therefore, be astonished if the greater proportion of the attempts made have produced works of an unsatisfactory character.

" In France, the art of architectural painting reached its culminating point in the twelfth century. The stained glass, the miniatures of manuscripts, and the fragments of mural decorations of that epoch announce an advanced state of art, singular comprehension of the value of colour and its harmonious arrangement, and a coincidence between that harmony and the forms of architecture.

" It is certain that the art of architectural decoration developed itself in the cloister, and proceeded from Greek Byzantine art. The most beautiful stuffs, furniture, decorated utensils, and a great number of illuminated manuscripts were then brought from the east, and were preserved in the treasuries and libraries of monastic establishments, and were used by the monks as models in their own art labours. Later on, towards the end of the twelfth century, when the practice of architecture was not exclusively confined to the monks, but was freely followed by laymen, a revolution took place in the art of painting, which, without being quite so radical as that which operated in architecture, modified to a considerable extent the principles laid down by the monachal school."

We have made a somewhat lengthy quotation from Mr. Viollet-le-Duc's able article on painting ; but we advise our readers not to rest satisfied with it, but to peruse the original article in its entirety.

Although we know absolutely nothing of the style or mode of executing decorative painting in England during the Saxon period, we have trustworthy information that painting was encouraged. We are told that so early as the year A. D. 674, Wilfred, bishop of York, had the walls, the capitals of columns, and the sacrarium arch of his church decorated " historiis et imaginibus et variis celaturam figuris ex lapide prominentibus et picturarum et colorum grata varietate. " (1) Bede informs us that Benedict Biscop brought over from France, at the termination of his visit in the year 678, paintings to decorate his abbey church, at Wearmouth. These were movable pictures executed upon wood tablets ; and consisted chiefly of portraitures of our Lord, the

(1) *Ricardi Prioris Hagustaldensis*, lib. I, cap. iii.

Virgin Mary, and the Apostles, with subjects from the Gospels and the Apocalypse. On a later occasion, in 685, he brought other paintings of a similar description, representing certain Scriptural types and antitypes, amongst which are mentioned Isaac bearing the wood on which he was to be offered up, and Christ bearing the cross; Moses lifting up the serpent in the wilderness, and the Crucifixion. There is little doubt that in the church where these pictures were placed, other and more permanent decorations were executed, such as those which adorned Wilfred's church at York. We are told that Biscop brought artists from France to teach the Saxons the art of making stained glass windows; it is highly probable that amongst these were included men skilled in mural decoration.

At the beginning of the ninth century the practice of decorating churches must have been common. At the second Council of Calcuth, in Northumberland, held in the year 816, a canon was issued requiring every bishop, before consecrating a church, to see painted on the walls or over the altar thereof a portraiture of the Patron Saint (1).

No direct mention is made in writings of this period (ninth century) of purely ornamental painting; but an examination of the superb illuminated manuscripts executed in this country, prior to the Norman invasion, impresses us with a highly favorable idea of the skill of the Saxons in ornamental art. One example may be here mentioned, the tenth century manuscript, in the possession of the Duke of Devonshire, known as the *Benedictional of St. Æthelwold*. In this book there is a peculiarly elaborate and richly coloured style of ornamentation, which might have been suggested by architectural painted decoration.

Mr. E. L. Blackburne (2), speaking of the paintings of the ninth and following centuries, in this country, says: — " Of the extent of the applications of painting and mosaic during this and the next succeeding century, little or no direct and authoritative record now exists, though indications of the adoption of such are to be traced in the descriptions of the altar Tabulæ and other similar gifts, made to the early Saxon church. Approaching the Norman era, however an extended use of ' picture work, ' under which term both these forms of decoration were at this time included, is decidedly and distinctly established. ' Superb picture work, ' intermixed with gold, is described as among the works performed by the Saxon archbishop, Aldred, to his cathedral of York in 1061 (3), and the pictured ornaments of the church of St. John, at Beverley, of a corresponding age, are also alluded to by the same authority. At a little later date, the second or Lanfranc's cathedral at Canterbury had its ceiling ' egregiè depictum. ' (4) Subsequently, Malmesbury also notices its ' pictured roof, ' (5) and in continuation, the choir paintings at Ely, by bishop Ridel (6), and the ceiling at Peterborough may be adduced, which

(1) " Every bishop shall draw the figures of the Saints to whom the church is dedicated either upon the wall, or on a board, or upon the altar." — *Synod. Calcuthens. apud Spelman Conc.* Vol. I, p. 327.

(2) In his interesting and valuable work, *Sketches, Graphic and Descriptive, for a History of the Decorative Painting applied to English Architecture during the Middle Ages* (London, 1847).

(3) *Chronica Pontificum Ecclesiæ Eboraci*, autore Thoma Stubbs Dominicano. This authority, speaking of the works of this bishop, says : " Totam ecclesiam a presbyterio usque ad turrim, ab intercessore suo Kinsio constructam, superbam opere pictorio, quod cœlum vocant, auro multiformi intermixo mirabili arte construxit. "

(4) *Chronica Gervasii.* " Cœlum inferius egregiè depictum' and ' cœlum ligneum egregiâ picturâ decoratum. "

(5) William Malmesbury, *de Gestis Pontif. Angl.*

(6) Bentham's *History of Ely*, p. 143, quoting Harleian MSS., Nos. 258 and 3721.

latter, erected according to general authority between the years 1177 and 1199, has descended (restored) to the present day."

The ceiling of the nave of Peterborough cathedral is the most important decorative work of the Norman period which has been preserved to our time. The ceiling is believed to have originally been flat; its present sloping sides and narrow vertical portions having been formed when the ceiling was raised, in the fourteenth century, above the newly-constructed pointed arches of the central tower. The painting of the flat portion of the ceiling, and the design of all save the narrow vertical sides, are of twelfth century date. The design consists of a series of lozenge-shaped compartments of two different proportions, alternating; the more elongated ones are painted on the flat central portion, and extend between the angles formed by the junctions of the sloping sides; the shorter lozenges are painted, partly on the flat and partly on the slopes, the angles passing through their centres. The lozenges are bordered with a bold design, chiefly composed of zig-zags of different kinds, with an inner fret, executed in dark brown and white. In the lozenges containing ornamental forms, the design is in white, outlined with black, and dotted and veined with red; the ground outside the design is green, and that inside it is red. These ground colours are counterchanged in the alternating lozenges, which contain foliated ornament. The lozenges along the central portion of the ceiling, and the alternate ones along the angles, are filled with seated figures of kings, bishops, saints, and curious allegorical figures, executed in colours, without the introduction of any gilding.

The designs bear every evidence of having been derived from early mosaic work; and it is probable that a similar and equally severe treatment characterised the mural decoration of the Norman period; it certainly would be a treatment perfectly in accord with the prevailing characteristics of Norman architecture.

Interesting remains of late Norman painting exist (now accurately restored) on the vault of the Jesus chapel, Norwich cathedral. The decoration is not so elaborate as that of Peterborough, but it bears evidence of a freer handling and a transition towards the scroll-work of the thirteenth century, a good example of which appears in the soffit of the arch in the same chapel. In the central point of the vault, which is without ribs or boss, is a square medallion, bordered by a narrow yellow band, outlined and dotted with black. Within this is a radiating foliated design, strictly conventional in character, executed in white, red, and green, outlined with black, and placed on grounds of red and chocolate-colour. A circle of yellow, outlined with black, divides the two ground colours, and interlaces with the several radiating members of the device. Painted bands extend from the medallion along the angles and crown-lines of the vault; those on the angles contain a lozenge diaper of a heraldic character, in red, green, white, and black; and those on the crown-lines are decorated with folded ribbons, strongly outlined with black, and shaded red and green on their different sides; the spaces formed by the ribbons contain black rings and dots. We here find a similarity between the decorative painting of the twelfth century and the illuminated ornaments of certain manuscripts of the same period. The latter frequently present folded ribbons and fret patterns shaded with different colour. The surface of the vault, within the bands, is covered with a perfectly plain brick pattern formed of single black lines on a white ground.

In France, the great cradle of Gothic art, decorative painting, prior to the time of Charlemagne, though probably correct in principle, was doubtless very simple in treatment. It was chiefly produced by firm lines, in black or some dark colour, applied directly to the surface of the stone, or more commonly on a white or buff coating of distemper, or *badigeon*, laid on to receive it. The lined ornamentation was afterwards enhanced in effect by the application of hatching or shading, in such colours as yellow, green, and red. White ornamentation, relieved with greenish or yellow touches, on dull red grounds, was frequently adopted. On the introduction of artists from Byzantium and Italy, by that patron of the arts, Charlemagne, decorative painting began an entirely new career in France. Progress from the art-schools of Charlemagne was steady and rapid, until the most complete development was reached at the close of the twelfth century. In Germany, also, architectural painting, inspired from the same source, was cultivated and practised with satisfactory results. There is no question that in the twelfth century painting and architecture found their most perfect and intimate union; the architect preparing for its reception, and the painter striving to accentuate and develop, by means of his lines, patterns, and colours, the constructive and ornamental features of the building. There is a great probability that in the generality of cases the architect and decorative artist were combined in one personage. If any true excellence is to be arrived at in our day in this branch of art, architects must study to design the painted decorations of their own buildings; and, further, they must poperly prepare for their reception. A church or other building, which is destined to be completed with a system of decorative painting, should be differently designed, so far as its interior is concerned, to one in which no painting is to be applied. This is a fact too often overlooked both in this country and abroad.

Throughout the thirteenth century the correct principles of architectural painting were maintained; although the architecture of the period did not present such favourable fields for its display as that of earlier date. In our opinion, no styles of architecture have lent themselves so thoroughly and consistently to the painter's brush as those which group themselves under the general term Romanesque. In them the large flat wall spaces, massive angular piers or circular pillars, capitals of the simple cushion form or sculptured with stiff conventional ornamentation, round arches with broad plain soffits, deeply sunk windows, wall arcades, simple bold mouldings, and the plain vaults or timber ceilings, all presented favourable fields for decorative painting which are not found in the lighter and more elaborately detailed pointed styles of the thirteenth and two following centuries.

Now we may conclude the present brief introduction with a few words on the general principles which governed the art of architectural decoration in the twelfth and thirteenth centuries; and which must govern it now if we desire to produce good consistent results.

All architectural decoration must be flat; that is, it must not, by any attempt at relief shading, interfere with the uniform surface to which it is applied. Objects may show gradations of colour after the manner of shading, but these must be conventionally rendered, without implying any definite line of light; and no cast shadows may be introduced under any circumstances. Under such a law of course all imitations or copies of objects in relief are impossible. When it is desired to introduce in painted decoration the semblance of features or details which truly belong to architecture, they must be rendered in such a manner as to satisfy the eye that no direct imitation or deception is aimed at. Reference to Plates XX., XXIV., XXV., XXVI., XXVII., and XXVIII. will fully explain our meaning.

Flat painting demands a peculiar treatment both as regards drawing and colouring; and this was thoroughly realised by the artists of the Middle Ages. The figures or forms represented must be rendered distinct by sharply defined outlines; those which are white or of some light tint upon a dark ground require no further definition; and the same remark applies to forms in dark colours on white or light grounds. When two or more light colours come together they must be separated by black or dark-coloured lines; and when dark or rich colours are associated they should be separated by gold or light lines. These rules were never lost sight of by the Middle Ages painters (1).

The colours to be used should be carefully selected with reference to the situation they are

(1) " La coloration subit des transformations moins rapides : l'harmonie de la peinture monumentale est toujours soumise à un principe essentiellement décoratif; cette harmonie change de tonalité, il est vrai, mais c'est toujours une harmonie applicable aux sujets comme aux ornements. Ainsi, par exemple, au XIIe siècle, cette harmonie est absolument celle des peintures grecques, toutes très claires pour les fonds. Pour les figures comme pour les ornements, ton local, qui est la couleur et remplace ce que nous appelons la demi-teinte; rehauts clairs, presque blancs, sur toutes les saillies; modelé brun égal pour toutes les nuances; finesse soit en clair sur les grandes parties sombres, soit en brun sur les grandes parties claires, afin d'éviter, dans l'ensemble, les taches. Couleurs rompues, jamais absolues, au moins dans les grandes parties; quelquefois emploi du noir comme rehauts. L'or admis comme broderie, comme points brillants, nimbes; jamais, ou très rarement, comme fond. Couleurs dominantes, l'ocre jaune, le brun rouge clair, le vert de nuances diverses; couleurs secondaires, le rose pourpre, le violet pourpre clair, le bleu clair. Toujours un trait brun entre chaque couleur juxtaposée. Il est rare d'ailleurs, dans l'harmonie des peintures du XIIe siècle, que l'on trouve deux couleurs d'une valeur égale posées l'une à côté de l'autre, sans qu'il y ait entre elles une couleur d'une valeur inférieure. Ainsi, par exemple, entre un brun rouge et un vert de valeur égale, il y aura un jaune ou un bleu très clair; entre un bleu et un vert de valeur égale, il y aura un rose pourpre clair. Aspect général, doux, sans heurt, clair, avec des fermetés très vives obtenues par le trait brun ou le rehaut blanc. Vers le milieu du XIIIe siècle, cette tonalité change. Les couleurs franches dominent, particulièrement le bleu et le rouge. Le vert ne sert plus que de moyen de transition; les fonds deviennent sombres, brun rouge, bleu intense, noirs même quelquefois, or, mais dans ce cas toujours gaufrés. Le blanc n'apparaît plus guère que comme filets, rehauts délicats; l'ocre jaune n'est employée que pour des accessoires; le modelé se fond et participe de la couleur locale. Les tons sont toujours séparés par un trait brun très foncé ou même noir. L'or apparaît déjà en masse sur les vêtements, mais il est, ou gaufré, ou accompagné de rehauts bruns. Les chairs sont claires. Aspect général chaud, brillant, également soutenu, sombre même, s'il n'était réveillé par l'or. Vers la fin du XIIe siècle, la tonalité devient plus heurtée; les fonds noirs apparaissent souvent, ou bleu très intense, ou brun rouge, rehaussés de noir; les vêtements, en revanche, prennent des tons clairs, rose, vert clair, jaune rose, bleu très clair; l'emploi de l'or est moins fréquent; le blanc, et surtout le blanc gris, le blanc verdâtre, couvrent les draperies. Celles-ci parfois sont polychromes, blanches, par exemple, avec des bandes transversales rouges brodées de blanc, ou de noir, ou d'or. Les chairs sont presque blanches. Au XIVe siècle, les tons gris, gris vert, vert clair, rose clair, dominent; le bleu est toujours modifié : s'il apparaît pur, c'est seulement dans des fonds, et il est tenu clair. L'or est rare; les fonds noirs ou brun rouge, ou ocre jaune, persistent; le dessin brun est fortement accusé et le modelé très passé. Les rehauts blancs n'existent plus, mais les rehauts noirs ou bruns sont fréquents; les chairs sont très claires. L'aspect général est froid. Le dessin l'emporte sur la coloration, et il semble que le peintre ait craint d'en diminuer la valeur par l'opposition de tons brillants. Vers la seconde moitié du XIVe siècle, les fonds se chargent de couleurs variées comme une mosaïque, ou présentent des damasquinages ton sur ton. Les draperies et les chairs restent claires; le noir disparaît des fonds, il ne sert plus que pour redessiner les formes; l'or se mêle aux mosaïques des fonds; les accessoires sont clairs, en grisailles rehaussées de tons légers ou d'ornements d'or. L'aspect général est doux, brillant; les couleurs sont très divisées, tandis qu'au commencement du XVe siècle elles apparaissent par plaques, chaudes, intenses. Alors le modelé est très poussé, bien que la direction une de la lumière ne soit pas encore déterminée nettement. Les parties saillantes sont les plus claires, et cela tient au procédé employé dans la peinture décorative. Mais dans les fonds, les accessoires, arbres, palais, bâtiments, etc., sont déjà traités d'une manière plus réelle; la perspective linéaire est quelquefois cherchée; quant à la perspective aérienne, on n'y songe point encore Les étoffes sont rendues avec adresse, les chairs très délicatement modelées; l'or se mêle un peu partout, aux vêtements, aux cheveux, aux détails des accessoires, et l'on ne voit pas de ces sacrifices considérés comme nécessaires, avec raison, dans la peinture de tableau. L'accessoire le plus insignifiant peint avec autant de soin, est tout autant dans la lumière que le personnage principal. C'est là une des conditions de la peinture monumentale. Sur les parois d'une salle vues toujours obliquement, ce que l'œil demande, c'est une harmonie générale soutenue, une surface également solide, également riche, non point des percées et des plans dérobés par des tons sacrifiés qui dérangent les proportions et les parties de l'architecture. " — M. Viollet-le-Duc, *Dict. de l'Architecture*, vol. vii.

to occupy in a building; and their depth of tone, or intensity of tint, should be graduated according to their distance from the eye, and the amount of light they receive. Pure colours, such as the primaries, red, blue, and yellow, should be very sparingly used in Gothic decoration; they are valuable, however, in salient lines or points of effect when associated with the secondary, mixed, or low-toned colours. We shall have more to say on this much-neglected but most important subject further on.

In arranging a system of decoration, the artist must be careful to keep it subordinate to the lines and architectural features of the building. In this respect the artists of the Middle Ages never fell into error. The strongest or most pronounced ornamentation must be confined to the lower portions of the walls, and applied to the most prominently marked lines and details of the building, such as the arches, bases, capitals, and mouldings generally. And, lastly, the entire system of decoration must be in perfect sympathy with the style of architectural and the motive it displays. If the building be of a lofty and refined character, such as the churches of the thirteenth and two following centuries, the decorations must be of a light and elegant type, in which the vertical or ascending elements are strongly marked. But if the building be of a Romanesque style, with low pillars, round arches, and bold horizontal mouldings, the decoration should be broad and massive in general treatment, in which severe patterns executed in low-toned colours should predominate.

Such, then, are the general principles which must be observed in architectural polychromatic decoration; and we may leave them at this point, as we shall have to allude to them again in the following and more practical part of our work.

PRACTICAL HINTS.

PROCESSES OF PAINTING.

Before proceeding to treat of the several kinds of polychromatic ornamentation suitable for buildings in the mediæval styles of architecture, and of the modes of arranging and associating the different patterns and ornaments on the walls, roofs, and the chief architectural features of such buildings, it is desirable that a few hints should be given with reference to the methods of painting commonly adopted, and the systems of colouring most to be recommended.

Of Fresco, and the recently introduced method of mural painting called Stereochromy, or Water-glass, it is quite unnecessary for us to speak in the present Work, as neither method would, under any ordinary circumstances, be resorted to in simple ornamental painting. The methods we shall briefly describe are Oil Painting, Tempera, and Wax Painting.

OIL PAINTING.

Oil painting is probably the best known and most popular method of painting adopted for the internal decoration of buildings of all kinds. But, though its processes are simple and the immediate results certain and satisfactory, there are several disadvantages connected with it which will always militate against its general adoption. The chief of these are — first, that all colours mixed with oil darken rapidly by exposure, and second, that the action of lime and damp are fatal to their durability. The rapidity and certainty of oil painting, and the fact of its being so generally understood, will always commend its adoption in works of an ordinary character.

Before proceeding to paint on plaster walls, it is absolutely necessary to ascertain that they are thoroughly dry, and to examine the nature and composition of the plaster. If the walls are not perfectly dry, oil paint must on no account be applied; and it is wise to bear in mind that under the most favourable circumstances no wall is in a fit state to receive it unless it has been finished above a year, including two summers. And, further, unless the wall is built of hard and well-burnt bricks, it is dangerous to calculate upon its dryness at any time; as a rule, a wall built of stone throughout may be considered unfit for the reception of oil painting.

In designing churches or other important buildings, which are destined to be completed with mural decoration, the architect should adopt special means to secure perfect dryness in the inner side of the walls. This in the generality of cases is best done by adding a facing of hard bricks, separated by a cavity from the main body of the walls, and bonded therewith simply by the stonework of the windows, doors, &c., and by bricks, dipped in hot asphalt, built in at intervals. A cavity of from one to two inches will be quite sufficient in ordinary cases.

Too much attention cannot be paid to the selection of materials for the composition of the mortar used in building the brickwork and for the plaster of the interior. The lime should be well slacked with pure spring water, and afterwards exposed for several weeks to the action of the air. The sand should be freshly dug from a pit, and be of a sharp crystalline character, and absolutely free from saline properties. The lime and sand should then be well ground together with fresh spring water.

It is almost unnecessary to remark that in all classes of painting, and particularly in oil painting, the very purest oils, spirits, varnishes, and pigments alone must be used.

TEMPERA.

Tempera, or what is more commonly designated Distemper Painting, is the most ancient of all the methods now used for mural decoration; and in some form or other it was with all probability the first that suggested itself when men began to decorate temples, dwellings, or tombs with colours. It consists simply of finely ground pigments mixed with water and some fixing or binding material, such as albumen, obtained from eggs, vegetable gums, or size, prepared from the skins of animals.

The Egyptians appear to have used tempera exclusively in the polychromatic decoration of their architectural and sculptured works, traces of colours fixed by wax having been found only on some portable objects and fragments of furniture. Their pigments, comprising blue, red, yellow, green, and black, all of remarkable durability, were simply mixed with glue or size, in all likelihood prepared from the skins of the wild animals of the Nile, the rhinoceros, hippopotamus, or crocodile. The peculiarly dry and uniform climate of Egypt was most favorable to the durability of tempera painting; so much so, that considerable remains of coloured ornamentation, executed between two and three thousand years ago, have been preserved to our day, in some instances almost as bright as when they were executed. Before applying the colours the Egyptians usually coated the stone with a fine and hard composition or gesso (1).

(1) " In Egyptian buildings, indeed, it sometimes happened that the shafts of columns were merely covered with white stucco, without any ornament, and even without the usual lines of hieroglyphics; and the same custom of coating certain kinds of stone with stucco was common in Greece. The Egyptians always put this layer of stucco, or paint, over stone, whatever its quality might be, and we are surprised to find the beautiful granite of obelisks and other monuments concealed in a similar manner; the sculptures engraved upon them being also tinted either green, blue, red, or other colour, and frequently one and the same throughout. Whenever they employed sandstone, it was absolutely necessary to cover it with a surface of a smoother and less absorbent nature, to prevent the colour being too readily imbibed by so porous a stone; and a coat of calcareous composition was laid on before the paint was applied. When the subject was sculptured, either in relief or intaglio, the stone was coated, after the figures were cut, with the same substance, to receive the final colouring; and it had the additional advantage of enabling the artist to finish the figures and other objects with a precision and delicacy in vain to be expected on the rough and absorbent surface of sandstone." — *The Manners and Customs of the Ancient Egyptians;* London, 1878, vol. ii, p. 286.

The Greeks, Etruscans, and Romans used tempera largely, although it appears that they preferred, for their higher class work, what has been called "encaustic painting," on account of its greater brilliancy, durability, and damp-resisting properties. In encaustic, wax and heat appear to have been the chief agents in fixing the colours. How the wax was used and the heat applied has not been made clear. In certain paintings, found at Pompeii, the colours seem to have been laid on with some aqueous vehicle, and afterwards protected by a thin coating of wax, applied in the form of a varnish, prepared by dissolving wax in some volatile oil. Heat was probably then applied by holding, at a safe distance from the surface of the painting, a brazier of burning fuel, or heated metal plates, and moving the same to different portions of the work until all had received sufficient heat to dispel the oil and melt the wax, so that it was readily absorbed by the porous surface on which the colours had been previously laid. By this process the colours would become enclosed within a thin film of pure wax. We shall have more to say on this subject when we come to speak of wax painting.

We may, however, now leave all matters relating to antique tempera, and proceed with our brief notes relative to the materials and processes adopted in the middle ages, about which there exists some definite information in the pages of old writers.

The materials which appear to have been almost exclusively used by the mediæval painters for tempering their colours were yolk and white of egg, gum, and glue; the first and second were probably adopted for special pigments or when the work was of small dimensions; the last for ordinary mural decoration. Glue, or a specially prepared size, continues to be used in the present day for tempera painting. The following remarks by Eastlake, with reference to English and German Tempera, are full of interest : — " Before entering on this subject, it may be necessary to explain the different meanings of the word *tempera*, applied to more or less liquid compositions. First, it is used in the general sense of mixture, in accordance with the import of the classic expression 'temperare' (thus Pliny, 'temperare unguentum'). In this widest application the Italian substantive 'tempera' means any more or less fluid medium with which pigments may be mixed, including even oil. Hence Vasari says, 'l'olio che è la tempera loro'. Secondly, in a less general sense, the term represents a glutinous, as distinguished from an unctuous or oily, medium; and thus comprehends egg, size, and gums; or, in a more general expression, binding substances originally soluble in water. Lastly, in its most restricted and proper acceptation, it means a vehicle in which yolk of egg is a chief ingredient : the varieties being yolk of egg mixed in equal quantities with the colour; yolk and white of egg beaten together, and diluted with the milky juice expressed from the shoots of the fig-tree; and the yolk alone so diluted. These last-named vehicles were the most commonly used by the painters of the South of Europe, before the invention and improvement of oil painting. They are described by the chief Italian writers on art, and by those who have followed them. Sandrart intimates that tempera was still employed in his time, but observes that it was only fit for dry situations (1).

(1) *Deutsche Acad.*, part. iii, p. 17., part. i, p. 66.

" Of the antiquity of the egg vehicle for the purposes of painting there can be no doubt, as Pliny speaks of the application of colours tempered with it on walls (L. xxxv. c. 26). The mixture of yolk of egg with the fig-tree juice is mentioned by the same writer, but with reference to medicinal purposes only (L. xxiii. c. 63). The fig-tree juice is noticed, in combination with other ingredients, by mediæval writers on painting; for example, in the Lucca MS. and in later treatises : a mode of procuring it is described in the *Secreti* of Rosello (1). Its omission in the Byzantine MS. (2) is probably accidental, as it is used by Greek painters of the present day. Dioscorides and Pliny remark that the juice of the fig-tree is of nature of vinegar, and that it coagulates milk (Diosc. l. i. c. 183. Plin. l. xxiii. c. 7). The modern use of vinegar, as a substitute for this juice, to dilute the yolk of egg in painting, is perhaps derived from these authorities. The tempera, composed of egg and fig-milk, or egg alone, used in dry climates, has been found to attain a very firm consistence, so as withstand ordinary solvents.

" Such was the nature of the Italian tempera properly so called. On walls, and for coarser work, warm size was occasionally used; but the egg vehicle, undiluted, was preferred for altar pictures on wood. Thus used, and drying quickly, it was difficult to affect a union of tints in the more delicately ' modelled ' parts of a work, — for instance, in the flesh, — without covering the surface with lines (tratteggiare; Anglice, hatching) in the manner of a drawing : Vasari indeed assumes that tempera pictures could not be executed otherwise. Examples of works, painted with the egg vehicle, being rounded and duly finished without this laborious process, are certainly not common in Italy. The pictures of Gentile da Fabriano and Sandro Botticelli are among the rare exceptions; an early specimen of Perugino, in the National Gallery, exhibits the dryer method. . .

" The general omission, by transalpine painters, of the juice of the fig-tree in the tempera vehicle (from the difficulty of procuring it, in colder climates, in sufficient quantity) is unimportant, as its use was by no means universal, even with the Italians. The mode in which the German and English artists retarded the drying of their vehicle, appears to have been by means of an ingredient which has re-appeared in our times in the manufacture of water colours, viz., the addition of honey. . . The use of honey, for the object above mentioned, by the Rhenish and English tempera painters, is proved by existing documents.

" A MS. in the public library at Strasbourg contains some directions for the preparation of colours and vehicles, among which the ingredient in question is named. The handwriting of the treatise is of the fifteenth century; but older authorities are quoted, and the practice generally described may belong even to the early part of the fourteenth century. The following passage is distinct as to its employment in painting : —

' I have now honestly, and, to the attentive, amply taught how all colours are to be tempered, according to the Greek practice, with two aqueous vehicles; also, how the colours are to be mixed, and how each colour is to be shadowed :

---

(1) *Della Summa de' Secreti universali;* Ven., 1575, vol. i., p. 127.
(2) *Manuel d'Iconographie chrétienne;* Paris, 1845.

[I have told] the whole truth. I will now teach how all colours may be tempered with size, on wood, on walls, or on cloth; and, in the first place, how the size is to be prepared for the purpose, so that it shall keep without spoiling, and also without an unpleasant smell. Take parchment cuttings, and, after washing them well, boil them in water to a clear size, neither too strong nor too weak. When the size is sufficiently boiled, add to it a basinful of vinegar, and let the whole boil well. Then take it from the fire, strain it through a cloth into a clean earthenware vessel, and let it cool. Thus prepared, it keeps fresh and good for a long time. The size being like a jelly, when you wish to temper any colours, take as much size as you please, and an equal quantity of water; mix the size and water together, and likewise much honey with them. Warm the composition a little, and inmix the honey thoroughly with the size. With this vehicle all colours are to be tempered, neither too thickly nor too thinly, like the other pigments of which I have already spoken. And these colours can all be coated with varnish; thus they become glossy, and no water or rain can then injure them, so as to cause them to lose either their tints or their shining appearance. '

" There is evidence to show that this receipt describes the practice of the English artists at a very early period, though that practice is here dignified with the epithet ' Greek.'

" A English document, in which the same ingredient is mentioned in connexion with materials for painting, belongs to the latter half of the thirteenth century. The notice occurs in an account of expenses relating to works executed by ' Master William ' at Westminster, and in the Mews at 'La Cherringe ' (Charing). . . .

" The accounts from which the following items are extracted comprehend the period from the second to the fifth year of the reign of Edward I. (1274-1277), but many are missing.

' To William the painter, and his associate, for the painting of twelve mews, 36s. To the same, for seven score and twelve lb. of green for the same, 75s. 4 $\frac{1}{2}$d. To Stephen Ferron, for twenty lb. of white, 2s. To the same, for one gallon of honey, 12d. Item : for one gallon of white wine, 3d. Item : for small brushes (?) and eggs, 3$\frac{1}{2}$d. Item : for yellow, 6d. Item : for size, 12d.' Other accounts relating to operations in the same locality include a variety of materials : but the surest indication that some of the work was of a superior kind is the frequent mention of eggs, the proper tempera vehicle for all finer painting.

" The use of wine in diluting glutinous vehicles was common for a long period. . . . The northern artists were sometimes content to use beer; the word (cervisia) is to be met with in early treatises on art; for example in Eraclius and Theophilus : its occurrence may perhaps be considered an indication of the transalpine origin of a MS., as it never appears in Italian documents. . . .

" With the exception of the peculiarities in practice that have been described, the technical processes in England during the fourteenth century closely resembled those of Italy. This is apparent, if we compare the records of the works executed at Westminster during that and the preceding age, with early Italian documents and treatises; the English methods occasionally indicate even greater precautions, chiefly with the view to intercept damp. Walls which were to receive paintings of figures appear to have been prepared with cloth glued over the surface : sometimes leaf-tin was found immediately next the wall, even under gilt plaster ornaments. Wood was generally covered either with parchment, leather, or linen. Plaster of Paris, the careful preparation of which for the purposes of painting is described by writers earlier than Cennini, was used for grounds. The common parchment size was employed for tempering the gesso or plaster, and as the ordinary vehicle for painting (with or without the addition of honey); the egg medium being reserved for finer work. This agrees with the practice of wall-painting described by Vasari when speaking of the ancient Italian methods. His words are : ' Walls, when dry, should receive one or two coats of warm size, the work being then executed entirely with colours tempered with it : and any one wishing to mix the colours with size will find no difficulty, observing the same general rule as in painting with yolk of egg : nor will the paintings be worse for being so executed.' "

The remarks, by Sir Charles Eastlake, which we have just quoted, ably epitomise all that is known relative to the materials used by the middle age artists in their tempera painting. That size, prepared from the untanned skins and the horns of animals, and from the skin and bones of certain fish, was the chief binding material employed in mural painting there can be little doubt; whilst for the finer portions or details, subsequently applied in completing the decorations, the egg medium was probably resorted to. Theophilus, who wrote during the eleventh century, gives the following receipt for the preparation of size for painting : —

" Take cuttings of the untanned skin of a horse or ass, dried, and carefully cut them up into small pieces, and taking the stag-horns, broken very small with a smith's hammer upon an anvil, place them together in a new pot, until it is half full, and fill it up with water, and so apply fire until a third part of this water is evaporated, so however, that it may not boil. And you will thus try it ; moisten your fingers with this water, and if, when they have become cool, they adhere together, the glue is good ; but if not, cook it until they do adhere together. Then pour this glue into a clean vessel and again fill the pot with water, and simmer it as before ; and do this four times. "(1)

In the manuscripts of Jehan le Begue we find a curious receipt for an aqueous vehicle, which may be here given, as translated by Mrs. Merrifield : —

" If you wish to make a water proper for distempering all colours, — Take a pound of lime and 12 pounds of ashes ; then take boiling water and put the whole together, making them boil well; after which let the mixture settle and strain it through a cloth ; then take four pounds of that water, heat it well, take about two ounces of white wax, and put this to boil with the water ; then take about $1\frac{1}{2}$ oz. of fish-glue, put it in water, and leave until it is well softened, and as it were melted, when you must manipulate it until it becomes like paste, and throw it into the water with wax, and make all boil together ; then add to it about an ounce and a half of mastic, and boil it with the other ingredients. Take some of this water on a knife-blade, or piece of iron, to ascertain whether it is done : if it is like glue, it is all right. Strain this water while hot or tepid through a linen cloth, let it settle, and cover it well. With this water you may distemper all kinds of colours. "

These remarks on the several preparations of the middle age artists cannot fail to be interesting to our readers : and the preparations might, with probable advantage, be tested by practical decorators. The use of the egg vehicle, and the introduction of honey in the manner described, might prove convenient under certain circumstances, and especially in works of a delicate or elaborate character.

The present desire for cheap materials, and those which are easily and quickly prepared, has done much to place distemper painting in an inferior position. It is unquestionably a

(1) Similar receipts are given in Cennino Cennini's *Treatise on Painting*, written in A. D. 1437. Engl. ed., London, 1844.

method of great value; and should be thoroughly studied by practical men with the view of obtaining the most durable results.

For good work, parchment size should be used, freshly prepared from shreds of parchment boiled in pure water. Of late years size has been specially manufactured for the ordinary distemper work executed by house decorators; but this should be well tested before it is employed in good decorative work.

The base of all light tinted grounds should be the finest gilder's whiting; this is prepared for use by being put into an earthenware vessel, covered with clean water, and allowed to stand until it is thoroughly saturated and the effervescence has ceased. The superfluous water is then poured off and the whiting is beaten up until it forms a smooth paste. The size is melted by heat and poured into the whiting; the whole is then stirred until the ingredients are thoroughly incorporated. The mixture is then allowed to stand for a day or so, until it sets as a weak jelly. In this state it is ready for use, only requiring to be well broken up and applied with a stiff brush. For tinted grounds the necessary colours must be added to the paste before the size is poured in. For rich coloured grounds whiting should be used with all pigments which admit of its addition. There are certain colours which are destroyed by the addition of opaque white, but as every decorator is familiar with these, they need not be mentioned here.

WAX PAINTING.

There is no doubt that of all the processes of mural painting, at all suitable for our climate, those which employ vehicles in which wax is incorporated are the best. Wax painting is unquestionably next to fresco in beauty and architectonic propriety of effect. It has much of its brilliancy; and closely approaches it in depth of tone, and that absolute freedom from gloss so essential in architectural decoration. So far as the action of air and moisture is concerned, wax is one of the most indestructible materials known; this and other highly favourable properties strongly recommend it to the attention of the decorative artist.

As we have already mentioned, the ancients employed wax largely in their decorative paintings. The Egyptians, however, do not appear to have used it for architectural works, but to have confined it to the preparation of colours for articles of furniture. The Greeks and Etruscans used it freely in the description of painting designated "encaustic." This, as the name implies, was a process in which heat was an active agent : how the heat was applied is not known, save that it was resorted to after the wax was laid on the wall. Its operation was evidently to melt the coating and warm the surface of the plaster, so that absorption could take place, and the pigments become firmly locked with the particles of the lime. It is not necessary to follow this method of painting to any length here, for any process requiring the application of heat must prove unsuitable for the decoration of buildings or large surfaces of any description; but the following remarks from the able pen of Mr. W. Cave Thomas cannot but be interesting to our readers : — "Ancient authors often make mention of

C

encaustic which, if it had been described simply by this word, signifying 'executed by fire,' one might suppose to have been a species of enamel-painting. But the expressions, 'encausto pingere,' 'pictura encaustica,' 'ceris pingere,' 'picturam inurere,' used by Pliny and other writers, make it clear that some other species of painting is meant. We have no ancient pictures of this description, and therefore the precise manner adopted by the ancients is not completely developed, though many moderns have closely investigated the subject and described their processes. At what time, and by whom, this species of painting was first invented is not determined by antiquaries, although it appears to have been practised in the fourth and fifth centuries. Count Caylus and M. Bachelier (a painter), were the first in modern times who made experiments in this branch of art about the year 1749. Some years after this, Count Caylus presented to the Academy of Painting at Paris his ideas and experiments on the subject of the ancient manner of painting in encaustic. In 1754 the Count had a head of Minerva painted by Mons. Vien after the process described by himself, and presented it to the Academy of Sciences in 1755. This induced Mons. Bachelier to recommence his experiments, with better success; but his manner of painting in encaustic differed from the ancient as described by Pliny, he did not therefore discover the real ancient manner; after this he made other experiments with the same object, all of which differed from the process as described by Caylus and others.

" Pliny, in a passage relating to encaustic painting, distinguishes three species. 1. That in which they used a stylus, and painted on ivory or polished wood (cestro in ebore), for which purpose they drew the outlines on the wood or ivory, previously saturated with some certain colour; the point of the stylus or stigma served for this operation, and its broad or blade end to clear of the small filaments that arose from the outlines made by the stylus in the wax preparation. 2. The next manner appears to have been where the wax, previously impregnated with colour, was spread over the surface of the picture with the spatula, the wax-colours being previously prepared and formed into small cylinders for use. By the side of the painter stood a brazier, which was used to heat the spatula with which the colours were smoothly spread after the outlines were completed, and thus the picture was proceeded with and finished. 3. The third method was by painting with a brush dipped into wax liquified by fire; by this method the colours attained considerable hardness, and could not be damaged either by the heat of the sun or the deleterious effects of sea-water. "

Mr. Thomas then proceeds to describe the several experiments and processes made and introduced by Chevalier Lorgna, Count Caylus, Mr. Werner, and Mrs. Hooker : but for these we must refer our readers to his interesting work, *Mural or Monumental Decoration*, from which the above quotation is made.

Of all the methods of using wax in decorative painting, that invented by Mr. S. Gambier Parry lays just claim to be considered the best and most convenient. This process was first brought before the public in article in the " *Ecclesiologist* " for March, 1863. He has named his process " Spirit Fresco, " and claimed for it the highest consideration, by pronouncing it to possess the following important qualities : — The luminousness of Fresco, the facility of Tempera, the richness of Oil Painting, and the durability of Encaustic. " All this," he says, " is to be obtained by a composition of wax, resins, and volatile oils, used in certain proportions and upon a definite system   My confidence is founded in great measure on the experience which art has afforded as to the nature and effect of those materials. Wax is an invaluable coating to the particles of colour, and is unaffected by the atmospheric changes of **heat** and cold, damp or dryness. It dries as it is used, both as to quantity and colour; not **like** oil, which darkens and becomes a mere thin horny pellicle on the evaporation of the water, which is the principal ingredient; nor like size, which is liable to peel off if used too thick, and to perish if used thin. But wax, although free from these objections, has weaknesses of its own. It is, however, most happily amenable to all demands upon it for mixture with other materials, which remedy its defects.

" Of all works of art which have been preserved to our times, none are in more perfect condition than those which have either been painted in, or protected by an oil varnish. That used in the earlier Middle Ages has in many cases darkened painfully, both from the faulty quality of the oil, and the choice of the resin (commonly sandarach) with which it was made up. But the protection afforded by it to the picture has been complete. A finer and harder resin not only protects better but darken less. That which was used by Van Eyck has protected his works perfectly, and has not darkened at all. The preparation used by his school was probably the same as we now have in the finest preparations of artists, copal. In wax painting, several other resins have been tried; but there are objections to most of them for the purposes of wall painting. Mastic, for instance, if used in sufficient quantities to consolidate and toughen the wax, becomes objectionable in another way by its gloss. It is also very hygrometric. Damara is in quality like a very poor edition of mastic, and liable to the same objections. The balsams do not mix well with the copal. But elemi resin will do so by heat, and when added in small proportions to wax, gives it the strength and toughness requisite for our purpose. If then we have a composition of these materials, wax, elemi, and copal, made sufficiently liquid by a fourth which is a solvent of the other three, namely, oil of spike, we have a medium perfectly applicable to wall painting in this climate; because it has strength to resist external damp, it is free from chemical action on the most delicate colours, it does not change by age; it is subtle enough to penetrate deeply the pores of the wall, and thus to key the pores of the painted surface to it; it is rich enough to protect the colours from the atmosphere and from each other; it is itself transparent, and dries with a dead surface. Whatever be the materials used, or methods of using them, where durability is the object, the one great point to be attained is some ready means of incorporating those materials with the wall itself, so that the painting may be made rather as it were into the wall than merely upon it. Fresco aims at this, by crystallization of the lime enclosing the colours in the drying plaster. Tempera aims at it by the adhesive qualities of the size, with which the porous surface of the wall is prepared. Encaustic aims at it by heat, driving the melted wax into the wall. Stereochromy attains it in a very slight degree, because the delicate shower of water (which must not risk the running of the colours on the perpendicular wall surface) is too fine to penetrate deeply into the pores as a more copious wash would do.

" By a modification of wax painting, a method may be obtained perfectly suitable to our climate by the durability of its materials, and to our light by its powers of colour to be as bright as the illuminations of a missal, or as sober as a Giottesque fresco. It is objected that wax deadens colours. This it need not do. The real objection to the common systems of wax painting, is that they reduce it to a slightly modified oil painting by mixing drying oils with the wax, and using colours ground up in the oil, or by the contrary fault of trusting the wax too much by itself, without strengthening it sufficiently with other materials.

" Another practice is to prepare the wall with wax, and then paint upon it with oil; this may do for mere decorative work, but for works of fine art its objections are manifest. To meet all requirements of wall-painting (where the walls are dry) with little risk of injury from the action of our climate, avoiding the objections to other systems and retaining all that is good and effective in them, I recommend the following scheme. Take a medium composed in these proportions :

Pure bleached wax. . . . . 3 oz.	}	by weight.
Elemi resin . . . . 1 oz.		
Oil of spike lavender . . . . . . 6 oz.	}	liquid measure.
Finest preparation of artists' copal. . 18 oz.		

which shall be used throughout from the first preparation of the wall to the last touch of colour laid upon it; that the whole mass may be perfectly homogeneous, all colours are to be ground up in it, and may be kept in tubes as oil colours are, or in any other way. The same composition diluted in twice its bulk of rectified spirits of turpentine makes the liquid with which the pores of the wall are to be saturated by copious washes. The number of these washes must depend on the absorbency of the wall surface, and the more absorbent that be the better. The last wash should be mixed up with :

Best gilders' whiting well washed and baked dry	}	three parts in bulk, not in weight.
Flake white ground (as usual) in water, and perfectly dry	}	one part ditto.

to the consistency of thin cream; the surface should be well covered with it, indeed, in most cases, two coats of this are better than one.

" Common rough wall plaster will take two doses of the transparent wash, and two with the opaque white. Each wash should be allowed twenty-four hours to evaporate. The object of these washes is to key the prepared surface deeply into the pores of the wall with a material which dries in them as hard as stone, and leaves a surface white, solid, absorbent, and of a good texture for painting. When the cartoon is traced on the wall, let a part of the design chosen be enough for a day's work, and washed over thinly with oil of spike, or highly rectified turpentine (the former is better, being a stronger solvent of the copal), the object being to open the surface which will then be painted into and dry into one solid mass, by the evaporation of the volatile oils. The wash should be lightly applied before the palette and colours are prepared for the day's work; the time thus employed will allow the surface to dry just sufficiently to let the paint be applied without dragging up and mixing with it.

" The vehicle for painting in which the brush must be dipped, must either be the same as the wall wash, only twice as much diluted, or oil of spike alone, or — when the cost of oil of spike is an objection, — highly rectified turpentine. The surface dries gradually, not skinning over as oil colours do, but equally throughout by evaporation. There are certain precautions to be taken which are essential, viz., not to touch any part with a volatile oil but such as is to be painted into, because those oils first melt the resins rather than the wax, and if left unpainted, will probably dry with a slight gloss which is very objectionable; but painting with a good body of colour into places thus softened, restores the unity of the materials and dries dead. There are also some peculiarities in certain colours which a little experience will soon ascertain. Cobalt, for instance, and ultramarine are naturally extremely dry, and require a fuller vehicle than many other colours; with them, therefore, plain volatile oil should not be used as a vehicle, but one composed of the medium diluted with three or four times its bulk of spike oil or turpentine. Ivory black dries badly. It is better to mix with it a fourth part of burnt umber, for all cases where black would otherwise be used alone. Some colours do very well in a thinner vehicle, such as emerald, oxide of chromium, lake, brown and rose madders, Indian and Venetian red, and others; these (mixed up of course with the medium mentioned at first) may be applied with a brush dipped in pure volatile oils. "

These directions are full, and convey a very clear idea of the valuable process introduced by Mr. Gambier Parry— a process of the greatest value to the mural painter. It has been fully tested by its inventor and others, and important works have been executed by it in Highnam church, Gloucester, and other buildings. It only remains for us to give Mr Parry's directions as to the preparation of the medium. He says:— " For the preparation of the medium, put first the elemi resin into a copper saucepan, and melt it gently over a charcoal fire or spirit lamp, the object being to evaporate from it the greater part of its essential oil. Then throw in the wax, and after that is melted, let the two ingredients simmer on together for ten minutes or so. Strain them through fine muslin to clear away the pieces of elemi bark or leaves, which if left to boil with the other materials would stain them a dark brown. Into the vessel to which the elemi and wax are strained add the oil of spike and the copal, and let them boil together, straining them a good deal until a white froth comes on the surface. They are them mixed and may be poured off into jars for use; the medium will not dry quite into a jelly. If that thicker form be required, it may be obtained by using half the quantity of spike oil and by boiling the whole two or three times, taking it off the fire each time, till the froth disappears, and then putting it on again. All this is in practice very little trouble, enough may be prepared in half an hour to last the artist for weeks of work. The only apparatus necessary is a strong spirit lamp or charcoal fire, and the copper saucepans, tinned inside; one, a small one, to melt the elemi and wax in — the other, a larger one, to mix and boil all the materials together. It is a good plan that these saucepans be made rather deep than broad, to avoid all access of the fire to the fumes of the materials. A long spoon for stirring, and a large graduated glass for measuring liquids complete the list of apparatus. "

Mr. Parry draws special attention to the necessity of using only the best and purest materials of their respective kinds; great care must be taken to procure the white wax free from all adulteration. That prepared for photography is the best to be obtained in the market under ordinary circumstances.

The chief objection against anything like a general adoption of the process is the expense of the medium; but for ordinary decorative painting—the branch of art we confine ourselves to in the present Work— a less expensive medium may be used. Mr. Parry informs us that highly rectified spirit of turpentine may be substituted for the oil of spike lavender, and that animi may be used instead of copal. With these materials the medium can be prepared at a moderate cost, and one quite compatible with first-class architectural decorative painting. Mr. Parry also adds that the elemi resin may be altogether omitted; but as he can give no good substitute for it, we are of opinion it should be retained.

We strongly recommend this process to the careful attention of decorators; for there can be no question as to its durability being far superior to both oil and tempera.

PREPARING THE DESIGN

AND

TRANSFERRING THE SAME TO THE WALLS OR OTHER PORTIONS OF A BUILDING.

Before proceeding to develop the scheme of the decoration, the artist should lay down on paper, to a uniform scale, the outlines of all the spaces and details which are to receive ornamentation; a scale of one inch to the foot may be accepted as generally convenient. On these outline drawings he should carefully develop the leading features of his scheme, which will in all probability divide the larger spaces into several compartments. The leading features will usually be in the form of horizontal and vertical bands or borders, crestings, archivolts, and medallions or fields for the reception of figures or figure subjects, or for some pronounced species of ornamentation which requires to be enclosed. When this is done, the artist should design the patterns suitable for the several compartments of the wall, and afterwards prepare the designs for the bands, crestings, &c., to accord with the patterns, and of such a style as to clearly mark their offices either as crestings or borders to special patterns, or as bands dividing two plain or ornamented compartments. The difference between a border and a band should be clearly understood. A border is a design which surrounds or encloses a pattern, and to which it strictly belongs, or which surrounds and frames a figure subject; it may accordingly be horizontal, vertical, circular, or curved in any form. A cresting, which is a description of border, can only be horizontal or raking. A band is a design, commonly enclosed within parallel lines, which may be placed horizontally, vertically, or inclined on a plain or patterned wall surface, around columns, across ceilings, or indeed on any portion of a building. Its use is simply to divide a surface; and when placed between two dissimilar patterns, it must be designed so as to be common to both; when repeated at regular intervals it forms a decoration very often used for the shafts of columns, or the lower divisions of wall surfaces.

The wall patterns, whatever their designs may be will group themselves under two classes of ornamentation, known as diaper-work and powderings. Diaper-work includes all patterns which are connected by certain general lines, or spring from some continuous feature, or which repeat so closely together as to produce a uniform effect of colour and an even distribution of pattern and ground. Powderings, on the contrary, are devices of an independent nature, repeated at regular distances, but not connected together by any link. The different treatments here alluded to are well illustrated by Plates VIII. and XI. The only description of pattern which may perhaps be considered to be outside both of the above classes of ornamentation, is that which was a great favourite with the artists of the middle ages, and is commonly known as the " brick pattern. " Examples are given on Plates II., III., IV., and V. Brick patterns are, however, strictly speaking, diapers; the difference between them and the more severe diapers being in some instances very slight, as may be seen by comparing Plates V. and XII.

The selection of the designs for the several spaces of the walls, as well as for the different portions of the building, is a matter which invariably requires careful consideration and study, not only with the view of avoiding a disturbed effect by the association of conflicting lines, but with the view of obtaining a proper balance of colour.

When the preliminary sketches are completed, the next step is the preparation of the full-sized drawings for the several designs. These should be drawn upon separate sheets of stout tough paper, large enough to contain each of the designs complete, with the necessary keys for registering the repeats. Vertical and horizontal lines should be distinctly drawn, through the axes of the patterns, to render their correct adjustment or register on the walls, &c., a matter of certainty. When a full-sized drawing is completed, it should be placed upon a board covered with common thin felt, with two or three sheets of moderately thick and very tough paper between it and the board, and fixed temporarily with drawing-pins or common tacks. Then, with a strong needle, fixed in a convenient handle, all the outlines must be carefully pricked through the several sheets, care being taken to hold the needle vertical in the process of pricking, so that the original dimensions of all the details may be preserved. The drawing may then be laid aside, and the pricked sheets used either for pouncing or for the preparation of stencils.

If the patterns are to be painted on the walls by hand, they must be transferred by pouncing. For this purpose one of the pricked sheets is to be taken, and the vertical and horizontal register lines drawn on it, as in the original design. Then the surface of the wall must be laid out with vertical and horizontal lines at the exact distances required by the pattern. These lines are readily laid on with a chalked cord, in the fashion usual with painters. The sheet is then to be placed against the wall, and fixed in position by strong needle-points, stuck in small wooden handles for the purpose; and briskly rubbed over all the pricked portions with a muslin bag containing some finely-ground charcoal, chalk, or Indian red, until enough of the powder has found its way through and clearly marked the outlines on the wall. The sheet is then moved onward the necessary distance required for the repeat, adjusted to the register lines, and pounced as before.

When designs are to be traced, it is not necessary to prick the original drawing, as it can be employed directly for the purpose, or a working copy can be made from it by placing it with a superimposed sheet of paper on a piece of glass fixed so that a strong light can strike through and show the lines distinctly. By this simple means an accurate copy may be quickly made. The paper used for tracing should be tough and thin, and the back well rubbed over with Armenian bole or some soft colour. The design must be fixed in its place, in the manner already directed, and the outlines gone over firmly with a blunt agate style. On removing the paper, the design will be found clearly transferred to the wall.

If the patterns are to be executed by stencilling, it is necessary to take one or more of the pricked sheets, and (after drawing on the necessary ties to keep all portions firmly together) cut out with a sharp-pointed knife, on a piece of plate glass, the portions to be executed in colour. The paper most suitable is a tough and highly rolled brown paper; and before it is used it should be well painted on both sides with shellac or knotting varnish. For small and delicate work a thick tinfoil is frequently used; the design has to be traced upon it with a moderately sharp point. When several colours are to be applied in different portions of the design, it is usual to prepare as many stencils as there are colours, each one having only the portions cut which belong to the colour in question. To secure perfect register it is best to employ what may be called the key or mother stencil, that is, one fully cut; from this any number of prints may be stencilled on the brown papers, and the separate portions cut out of each. The absolute certainty of accurate register is by this simple means secured, and any damaged stencil can readily be replaced. Each stencil should have several small pieces belonging to the other colours cut out to serve as register marks. Designs which are to be executed by stencilling should have as many natural ties as possible, and the different colours should have a clear space of the ground left between them. As few accidental ties should be introduced as possible, for they have to be filled up immediately afterwards by hand or small special stencils.

EXECUTING THE DESIGN.

Although no one would attempt to paint the walls of a church or dwelling-house without some general knowledge of the art, yet a few hints here may not be out of place. They shall be extremely brief.

In executing ornamental designs by hand, that is with the free brush, considerable skill is required, not for the simple laying on of the colours, but in giving that artistic freedom and feeling which are readily felt when seen, but which are almost beyond description. It is this freedom and feeling which renders moderately good hand painting superior to the finest stencilling.

The slight differences of intensity in the colouring, which take place at every fresh charge of the brush, impart a great softness to the general effect, and should be rather studied than avoided. Indeed, with the view of aiding this, the artist should provide himself with two or more tones of each colour, to be used at pleasure as his taste directs. The effect of this is shown in the leaves on Fig. 2, Plate XXXI. In applying the colours, the brush should be used as much as possible in the direction of the design; in flowers, from their centres towards their edges; in leaves, from their stems to their points, or from their mid-ribs to their edges; in scrolls, stems, and such like, the brush should simply follow their curves. Of course there are many portions of decorative designs which demand flat painting, such as those shown on Plate XXIV.; and all coloured grounds on which designs are to be executed must be perfectly uniform.

Broken colour is quite as valuable in decorative painting executed by stencilling as in that done by the free brush. This fact is not generally known or realised; on the contrary, it is commonly supposed that one of the chief merits of stencilled work is its perfect flatness and uniformity of colour. So much, however, is the reverse of this the case that rich decorative painting executed with uniform colours never fails to have an inartistic and painfully hard effect. Broken colours are most valuable in floral and scroll work designs, such as those shown on Plates V., XVI., XVII., XVIII., XXX., and Figs. 2 and 3, Plate XXXI. It may also be skilfully used in such designs as those represented on Plates XXVI., XXVII., and XXVIII. The great expense which attends elaborate chromolithographic printing has prevented our indicating broken colouring on these plates.

Before proceeding to stencil a pattern which is to be rendered in broken colours, at least three tones of each colour should be prepared, the middle tones being the normal ones, or, in other words, those which would be adopted alone for flat stencilling. For example, let us take the flowing designs of the bands, Figs. 1 and 2, Plate XVII. The normal colours are those given in Nos. 4, 12, and 18 on Plate I; and from these three another six have to be prepared, by the addition of pigments which will darken and lighten them. Two portions of the red are poured into separate pots; and to one is added some bright yellow ochre, to incline it towards an orange; and to the other a little Indian red and black, until it approaches the colour No. 6. The green is divided in like manner, and lightened by the addition of yellow and white, and darkened by the addition of burnt sienna and a little Prussian blue. The blue is divided, and lightened with white and a very small proportion of green, and darkened by Prussian blue. When these are ready, nine stencil brushes are taken, charged with the different colours, and used as the skill and taste of the artist may direct. The centre portion of a leaf may be put in with the lightest green, the end where it springs from the stem with the middle tone, and the point with the darkest : in stencilling quickly there is no difficulty of blending one tone into another, so that no hard edges or sudden

D

gradations may appear. The next green leaf may, and indeed should, be treated in a different way, the tones being altered in position; no attempt should be made to stencil two leaves exactly alike. The other colours should be treated after the same manner. A little experience renders this mode of stencilling perfectly easy and certain. All margin lines or continuous horizontal designs, such as those which bound the bands alluded to, should be of uniform colours, otherwise the composition will lack force and distinctness. Lines are invariably drawn by hand with a brush and straight-edge.

In the class of decorative painting which is treaded of in the present Work, bright or crude colours should be avoided as much as possible. The primaries, represented by chrome yellow, vermilion, and ultramarine; and the secondaries, represented by orange chrome and deep emerald green, should be used only in the smallest possible quantities. With the occasional use of a red approaching vermilion, all these colours are absent from our Plates, The yellows most valuable for decorative painting are the ochres, which vary from a bright· though not vivid, yellow to a colour nearly approaching a tawny brown. The finest kind is that known as Oxford ochre; it produces beautiful quiet tints with white and other colours, including valuable greens when combined with Prussian and other blues. In combination with vermilion, Indian and Venetian reds, it produces refined and quiet colours of great value.

The most useful reds are light red, Indian and Venetian reds; these may be brightened to any required degree with vermilion. The three reds produce good ground colours when mixed with white, white and yellow ochre, or white and black. Lake and vermilion produce a rich crimson; and lake, vermilion, and Venetian or Indian red yield colours of great intensity.

Of all the blue pigments (setting aside genuine ultramarine), blue ochre is the most permanent, and Prussian blue the most generally useful. These are of the greatest value in preparing durable greens; and produce pleasant toned light blues when combined with white. Cobalt blue is also highly to be recommended for the preparation of clear light blues. The finest smalt blue is a most durable and useful pigment, being unaffected by lime. We may mention that, as a general rule, blues with a slight greenish tint are more pleasing in decorative painting than those which incline towards purple.

The greens used for decorative painting should as a rule be mixed pigments, that is, composed of blues and yellows; permanent colours being in all cases used. The ordinary green colours of commerce cannot be depended on. Bright or what may be designated spring greens are seldom introduced in decoration, being too hard and forcible; but all the tones of greens as found in autumnal foliage are highly suitable. Such greens may readily be produced with Prussian and cobalt blues and the permanent yellows — the ochres, lemon yellow, and raw and burnt sienna. To compounds of these, Indian and Venetian reds, Vandyke brown, and burnt umber may be added to produce the more sombre tones required. All the greens may be brightened with white or lemon yellow according to the character of the tint desired.

It is unnecessary for the purposes of the present Work to go further into detail on matters relating to colours, but we cannot do better than conclude our brief remarks by giving the following two lists of reliable pigments from Field's *Chromatography* (1).

TABLE A.

" Pigments, not at all or little liable to change by the action of light, oxygen, and pure air, nor by the opposite influences of shade, sulphuretted hydrogen, damp and impure air ; nor by the action of lead or iron.

WHITE	Zinc White. True Pearl White. Constant or Barytic White. Tin White. The Pure Earths.	PURPLE	Gold Purple. Madder Purple. Purple Ochre.
YELLOW.	Yellow Ochre. Oxford Ochre. Roman Ochre. Sienna Earth. Stone Ochre. Brown Ochre. Platina Yellow. Lemon Yellow.	RUSSET	Russet Rubiate, or Madder Brown. Intense Russet. Orange Russet.
RED.	Vermilion. Rubiates, or Madder Lakes. Madder Carmines. Red Ochre. Light Red. Venetian Red. Indian Red.	BROWN AND SEMI-NEUTRAL. . . .	Vandyke Brown. Rubens' Brown. Bistre. Raw Umber. Burnt Umber. Marrone Lake. Cassel Earth. Cologne Earth. Antwerp Brown. Hypocastanum, or Chesnut Brown. Asphaltum. Mummy, &c. Phosphate of Iron. Ultramarine Ashes. Sepia. Manganese Brown.
BLUE	Ultramarine. Blue Ochre.		
ORANGE.	Orange Vermilion. Orange Ochre. Jaune de Mars. Burnt Sienna Earth. Burnt Roman Ochre. Damonico. Light Red, &c.	BLACK	Ivory Black. Lamp Black. Francfort Black. Mineral Black. Black Chalk. Indian Ink. Graphite.
GREEN.	Chrome Greens. Terre-Verte. Cobalt Green.		

REMARKS. — This Table comprehends all the best and most permanent pigments, and such as are eligible for water and oil painting. "

(1) *Chromatography; or a Treatise on Colours and Pigments, and of their Powers in Painting*, &c., by George Field ; London, 1835.

TABLE B.

" Pigments which are little or not at all affected by *lime,* and in various degrees eligible for fresco, distemper, &c.

WHITE . . . . . .
{
Barytic White.
Pearl White.
Gypsum, and all
Pure Earths.
}

YELLOW . . . . . .
{
Yellow Ochre.
Oxford Ochre.
Roman Ochre.
Sienna Earth.
Di Palito.
Stone Ochre.
Brown Ochre.
Indian Yellow.
Patent Yellow.
Naples Yellow.
Massicot.
}

RED . . . .
{
Vermilion.
Red Lead.
Red Ochre.
Light Red.
Venetian Red.
Indian Red.
Madder Reds.
}

BLUE . . . .
{
Ultramarine.
Smalt, and all
Cobalt Blues.
}

ORANGE . . . . . .
{
Orange Vermilion.
Orange Lead.
Orange Chrome.
Laque Mineral.
Orange Ochre.
Jaune de Mars.
Burnt Sienna Earth.
Damonico.
Light Red, &c.
}

GREEN . . . . . .
{
Green Verditer.
Mountain Green.
Chrome Green.
Mineral Green.
Emerald Green.
Verdigris, and other
Copper Greens.
Terre Verte.
Cobalt Green.
}

PURPLE . . . . . .
{
Gold Purple.
Madder Purple.
Purple Ochre.
}

BROWN AND SEMI-NEUTRAL . . . .
{
Bone Brown.
Vandyke Brown.
Rubens' Brown.
Bistre.
Raw Umber.
Burnt Umber.
Cassel Earth.
Cologne Earth.
Antwerp Brown.
Chesnut Brown.
Asphaltum.
Mummy.
Ultramarine Ashes.
Manganese Brown.
}

BLACK . . . .
{
Ivory Black.
Lamp Black.
Frankfort Black.
Mineral Black.
Black Chalk.
Indian Ink.
Graphite.
}

PRINCIPLES OF DECORATIVE DESIGN AND COLOURING.

The principles of design which should guide the artist in selecting and arranging patterns for the decoration of the walls and other portions of the interior of a church are few and simple; probably the most important one is, that no ornament or disposition of lines should be adopted which are calculated to interfere with the structural features of the architecture, but, on the contrary, everything should be designed with the view of accentuating and en_riching them. True architectural decoration is an integral part of architecture, and should grow out of it, assisting its expression and beautifying its constructive elements.

In the decoration of walls, their flatness and solidity must be recognised, and no attempt must be made to destroy the appearance of either. All effects of relief or depression should be avoided in whatever ornament is applied. Walls which rise from the floor may be divided horizontally into two or more spaces, each of which may be differently treated. As a rule, that nearest the floor should be kept as solid and quiet in design and colour as possible, serving as a foundation for the lighter and more delicate enrichments above. Deep-toned plain colours, such as Nos. 6, 8, 9, 11, 12, and 18, on Plate I., are frequently used; but it is very advisable, on the score of beauty and less liability to show injury, that some sort of pattern should be added, either in darker or lighter colours. Such patterns as the four given on Plate II., and Nos. 3 and 4 on Plate III., are highly suitable for such a purpose. Mr. Viollet-le-Duc made good use of designs and colouring of a similar nature, in his decoration of the chapels of the cathedral of Notre-Dame, at Paris. On Plate VI., four designs of a different style are given; Nos. 1 and 2, on account of their hard and marked treatment, should be restricted to surfaces of moderate extent. The same remark applies to the four designs on Plate VII., which, if executed in deep low-toned colours, would be suitable for the lower portions of walls. It is not often that light grounds and elaborate ornamentation are adopted so near the floor, but such may occasionally recommend themselves to the artist. Patterns of a severe nature, such as those given on Plate V., are highly suitable; they may be executed in any colouring upon light-tinted grounds. When the lower division of a wall is of a considerable height, and a rich and uniform effect is desired, brocade patterns and powderings are very suitable. The brocades given on Plate VIII., executed in two tones of any colour, are probably of the best class for this purpose; while those on Plate X., in gold on deep grounds, are suitable for the walls of chancels; or spaces of small extent, as mentioned in the description of the Plate. The collection of powderings on Plate XI. illustrates the several kinds which have been commonly used by Gothic artists. For remarks on their different treatments, see the description of the Plate. Rich diaper patterns in gold on deep grounds, such as those on Plate XIV., are also suitable for the walls of chancels.

When the dado (the term commonly employed to distinguish the lower part of a wall when it is differently treated from the upper or general wall surface) is of a plain colour, it may be finished, on its upper edge, either by one or more lines of colour, or with a border or band of some simple design, after the fashion of Nos. 7, 8, and 9, Plate XIV. The colouring of the border should be of such a nature as to artistically unite the dado colour and that of the wall above.

Considerably more freedom may be used in the decorations of the upper portions of the walls. They may be of a uniform vellum or other light tint, simply relieved by ornamental bands placed at such intervals or in such positions as the architectural features — arches, windows, doors, &c. — may dictate. On walls pierced with windows, a band may appropriately be run immediately under the springing line of their arches, and another one midway between it and the border of the dado, which latter will, in all probability, be immediately under the sills of the windows. When the general surface of the wall is plain, the bands should be of a light and graceful character, executed on the same tint as the wall, or on a ground a little darker. Bands as Nos. 1, 3, 5, and 6, Plate XVI., the five on Plate XVII., and Nos. 1, 3, and 5 on Plate XIX., are of the several types best adapted for plain walls; designs of a heavier nature would appear too pronounced.

Simple brick patterns were much used by mediæval decorators; and where a light system of wall decoration is required, nothing can be more appropriate or of better architectural character. Specimens of these in their simpler forms are given in Nos. 1 and 2, Plate III., and Nos. 1, 2, 4, and 5, Plate XXI., surrounding the medallions. More elaborate varieties appear on Plates IV. and V.; the latter are of too rich a character to be carried over large surfaces.

Next to the brick patterns come the variety of skeleton diapers illustrated on Plate XII. These, however, do not admit of being used to the same extent as the simpler brick patterns; but their effect is both rich and pleasing in confined spaces where brick patterns are hardly appropriate.

Brocade patterns, such as are given on Plate IX., are highly suitable for large surfaces of walls, especially when executed in monochrome, as shown on the Plate. If greater richness is desired, such patterns may be stencilled in low-toned broken colours, with very satisfactory results. Brocades are best for wall spaces which are not cut up with horizontal bands; they do not require boundary lines of any kind, and are adapted to surfaces of any shape.

When decoration of a symbolic or heraldic nature is desired, powderings become convenient and appropriate. Mr. Viollet-le-Duc has introduced them largely on the upper wall spaces in the chapels of Notre-Dame, where they are almost invariably of a symbolic character, or in the form of monograms. How the symbols, emblems, and monograms may be simply treated is shown in Nos. 7, 9, 10, 11, and 12, Plate XI.; heraldic devices appear in Nos. 4 and 6. Powderings may be stencilled in any colour or colours upon light grounds, and in any situation on a wall, plain or banded. For further details, see the description of Plate XI.

It is not our intention in the present Work to go into the question of pictorial or figure decoration; that, along with the higher class of ornamental enrichment, may form the subject of an independent Work at a future date; but we may remark that where single figures, such as angels bearing symbols or inscriptions, or small subjects, are to be introduced, medallions or spaces, enclosed by borders, should be provided, after the fashion of those on Plate XXI., Nos. 3, 4, 5, and 6. Ornamental medallions, as Nos. 1 and 2, are frequently introduced between arches, windows, &c., to relieve the monotony of the wall surface. When large standing figures have to be enclosed, it is advisable to introduce canopies, supported on pillars; of course these have to be conventionally rendered. Materials are given on Plates XXIV., XXVI., XXVII., and XXVIII., from which such features may readily be composed. A succession of single figures may appropriately be placed in an arcade, such as No. 2, Plate XXV.

In decorating large spandrils, such as those between the main arches of a church and the clerestory walls, the same principles as those which should guide the treatment of the upper surfaces of general walls are to be observed. The surface of the spandrils may be reduced by surrounding the arches with a border, of radiating or flowing design. When the ground is of brick pattern, a simple border, such as that round the medallion No. 1, Plate XXI., is most appropriate, or something of the fashion of No. 6, Plate XVI., would answer well. Medallions containing ornamental devices or figures are frequently placed in the centre of spandrils, the grounds round them being of brick pattern, diaper-work, brocade pattern, powdering, or covered with scrollwork or foliage.

In elaborate schemes of decoration, the mouldings of all arches should be entirely or partially coloured. As mouldings are so varied in their contours and number of members, it is impossible to give directions as to their polychromatic treatment beyond the most general hints. Large splays or flat members may have simple ornaments added to them; bold hollows and projecting rounds should be painted with quiet harmonious colours accentuated by fillets of white, black, or gold. Small round members may be gilded or relieved with a plain spiral, as shown in No. 3, Plate XXXI.; but a treatment of this kind should be avoided on large round members, and never executed in bright colours, as the result is certain to be inartistic if not absolutely vulgar. What we have said of arch mouldings is equally applicable to all other mouldings.

The mediæval artists frequently decorated the shafts of pillars; and several traces of their designs have been preserved. They usually preferred designs of a spiral or zig-zag nature, as neither appeared to destroy the vertical feeling of the shaft. Plate XXII. are given nine patterns developed in accordance with ancient principles. The designs on Plate XXXIII. are of the richest class of column decoration, executed in black, blue, red, and green upon gold grounds. This class has been adopted for the pillars in the Sainte-Chapelle, at Paris. The very common use made of polished granite and marble for the shafts of pillars in modern Gothic buildings has prevented polychromatic decoration being much resorted to in connexion with the feature. The best examples of modern column decoration, after ancient models, are probably those executed, under Mr. Viollet-le-Duc's direction, in the chevet of the abbey of Saint-Denis; but, like the generality of modern French church decorations, they are rather crude and forcible in colour.

When the shafts of pillars are decorated, it is usual to apply colour also to the bases and capitals; but great caution is necessary in decorating the latter, especially when they are sculptured. During the middle ages colour was freely applied to sculpture of all descriptions, but in the present day there appears to be great reluctance to follow this ancient practice in its full development. There seems to be too great a value laid upon stonework nowadays; for where it appears in the interiors of our churches it is respected to such an extent as to be denied the advantages of decoration. The generality of modern schemes of polychromatic decoration are entered on with a timidity and half-heartedness which secure their failure in nine cases out of ten. Usually the decoration is confined to the plastered surfaces, the stone work and woodwork being left untouched. That such was not the case in the great periods of Christian architecture we have ample proof. When it is considered expedient or desirable not to entirely cover stonework with painting, it should be saturated with a transparent medium, so as to fill up the pores and protect its surface, and then any ornaments may be painted upon it, or its mouldings and other salient portions may be enriched with colours and gilding. These remarks apply equally to all architectural features, pillars, with their bases and capitals, arches, cornices, and string-courses, door and window jambs and arches, window tracery, and all descriptions of sculptured work.

On Plate XXIX. are given seven designs for the decoration of the soffits of beams, purlins, and rafters, representative of the more appropriate styles : and in Plate XXX. are four designs for different styles of ornamentation applied to the spaces between the rafters of open timber roofs; to which are added further devices for the faces of rafters. On roofs of large dimensions, painting executed in monochrome, such as shown in No. 1, has a quiet and agreable effect; the patterns may either be of the form given in this example, several different flowers being introduced to avoid undue monotony of effect, or of the brocade type such as those given on Plate IX. Patterns of the same nature as No. 3, Plate XXX., may also be rendered in monochrome; two designs should be adopted, alternating with each other to prevent monotony.

On Plate XXXI. are illustrated the more characteristic and appropriate styles of decoration for the numerous curved members of open timber roofs. No. 3 is suitable for early pointed work; Nos. 1 and 2 for middle pointed roofs; and the remaining examples are of a late character.

We have now said sufficient for the purposes of the present Work, and to enable both the decorative artist and amateur to understand our series of designs. We have developed these designs with the chief aim of supplying diversified models, full of suggestiveness to the artist; and as the number of plates was of necessity limited, we have confined ourselves to the illustration of the more generaly useful class of decorations for buildings in the Gothic styles. In a future Volume we may illustrate the more elaborate sections of our subject.

THE END.

PLATE I.

COLOURS AND TINTS MOST SUITABLE FOR DECORATIVE PAINTING.

The use of pure or positive colours in mural and other decorations is much to be condemned, especially in ecclesiastical structures and domestic buildings in the mediæval styles. Such garish pigments as vermilion, ultramarine, emerald and green, and the chrome yellows, have during late years been freely used, to the utter destruction of repose and artistic effect. Such works as the interior decorations of the Sainte-Chapelle, at Paris, and the modern church of Notre-Dame de Bon-Secours, near Rouen, are examples of the injudicious use of crude and too brilliant colours, resulting in an extremely garish effect in both cases.

The colours and tints given on this Plate are all mixed or modified; and, except in very special works, are appropriate and sufficient for all architectural decorations. They are adhered to throughout all the designs in the present Work.

Plate I

W & G AUDSLEY, INVEN. ET DEL.

Imp. Firmin-Didot & Cie, Paris

PLATE II.

The four designs on this Plate, in their deep and sombre colouring, are very appropriate for the decoration of the lower portions of the side walls of churches or large halls. These designs may have their colouring reversed if preferred, or for the sake of variety. Patterns Nos. 1, 2 and 4 may have their lines and devices executed in dark colours on grounds several shades lighter, as in No. 3. The latter may, in like manner, be carried out with a light pattern on a dark ground.

These designs, as coloured on the Plate, are most suitable for dados or positions where a supporting effect is desired; but if they are carried out similar to Patterns Nos. 1 and 2 on Plate III., with dull red, brown, or green lines, etc., on light tinted grounds, they become suitable for the upper portions of walls, above plain dark-coloured dados, or for covering large surfaces which admit of such a style of decoration.

Nos. 2, 3, and 4 are based on the ordinary " brick pattern," with single horizontal and vertical joint lines. No. 1 is of the simplest treatment with the introduction of double vertical lines.

Plate II

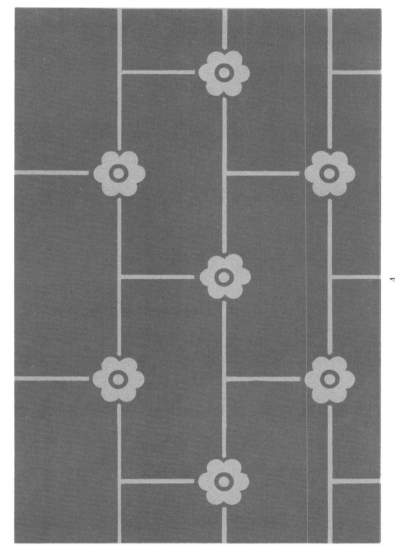

2

4

1

3

W & G AUDSLEY, INVEN. ET DEL.

Imp. Firmin-Didot & Cie, Paris

PLATE III.

PATTERNS ON LIGHT AND DARK GROUNDS FOR THE UPPER AND LOWER PORTIONS OF WALLS.

———◇———

This Plate presents another series of simple designs, based on the ancient " brick pattern." The remarks made on the previous designs (Plate II.) apply generally to these also, particularly as regards the reversing of the colours. No. 1 is the simplest form of this system of wall enrichment; and may be used over any large surface which is not required to be brought prominently forward in the general scheme of decoration. It is similar to No. 1, Plate II., in design; but its lines are dark on.a light ground instead of light on a dark ground, a treatment which renders it suitable for large surfaces and the higher portions of walls. No. 2 differs from the preceding in having double horizontal joint lines instead of double vertical ones; and here a quaint diagonal dash breaks the oblong space of each division without materially altering the severity of the simpler treatment. No. 3 shows another method of breaking the hard uniformity of the oblong spaces. The patterns shown in designs Nos. 1 and 5, Plate XXI., indicate ancient methods adopted with a similar intention. No. 4 has both double horizontal and vertical joint lines, and shows the simplest method of enriching the brick pattern by a central device in each of the divisions. The form and colouring of the device admit of endless variety. Here the fancy of the artist need be his only guide. Care should be taken, however, not to make the device larger in proportion to the oblong division than is shown on the present example.

Plate III

2

1

4

3

W & G A U D S L E Y , I N V E N . E T D E L

I m p . F i r m i n - D i d o t & C i e , P a r i s

PLATE IV.

ELABORATE PATTERNS FOR WALLS, IN RICH COLOURS UPON LIGHT GROUNDS.

———————————

The two designs on this Plate are based on the brick pattern; and show different methods of enriching the oblong divisions with scroll-work, issuing from the vertical and horizontal joint lines. The methods here illustrated can be varied to any extent, both as regards detail and colouring. It is only necessary to keep the main lines of the scroll-work the colour of the joint lines out of which they spring. Patterns such as these can only be properly executed on light grounds; but of course the ground tint may be any shade of buff, grey, green, blue, &c.

These designs may be carried over large surfaces of wall, but their richness rather limits their use. They are very suitable for the lower portions of walls, being carried up from, say, eight to fifteen feet, as the case may dictate. The wall above should be of a plain tint, and the pattern should be divided from it with a cresting or band, such as are shown on the Plate.

Instead of the gold introduced in the designs, a gold-colour or some other harmonious colour may be used.

The following Plate presents more elaborate patterns of a similar character to those above described.

Plate IV

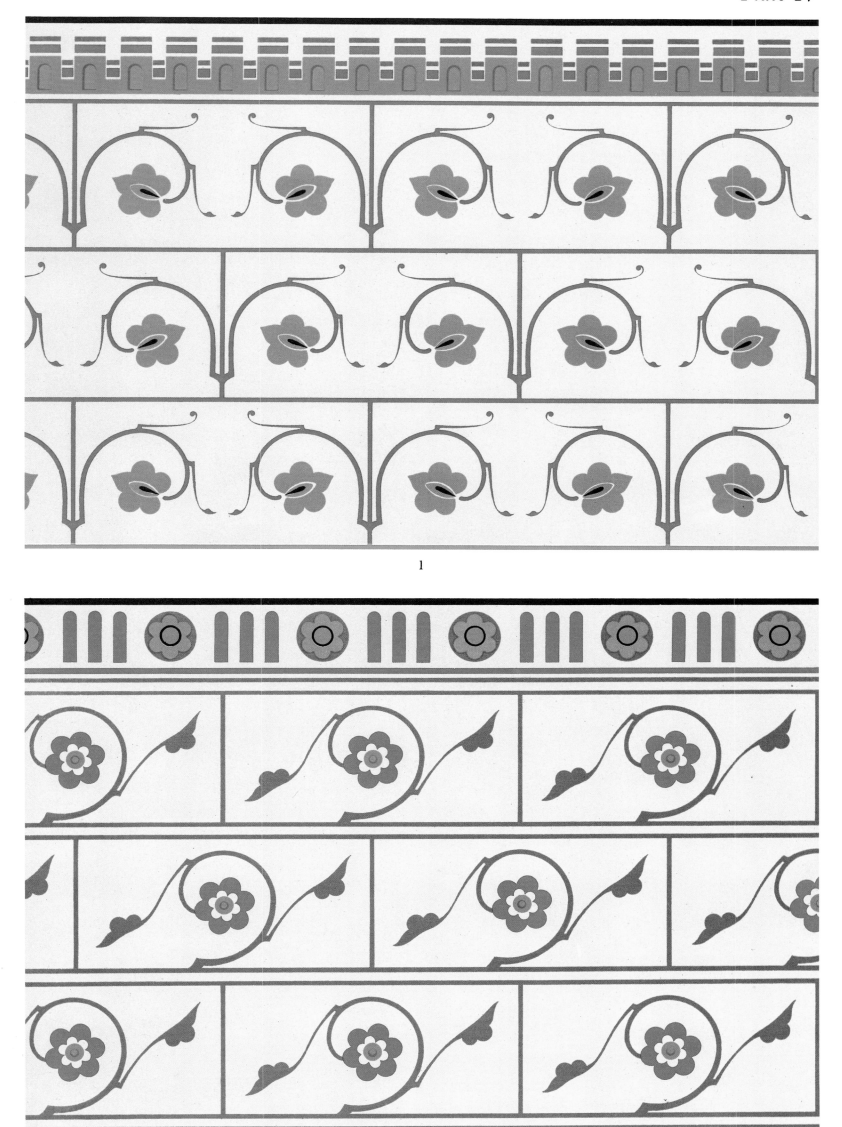

1

2

W & G AUDSLEY, INVEN. ET DEL.

Imp. Firmin-Didot & Cie, Paris

PLATE V.

ELABORATE PATTERNS FOR THE LOWER PORTIONS OF WALLS,
EXECUTED IN RICH COLOURS ON LIGHT GROUNDS.

The four designs on this Plate present the most elaborate treatments which the severity of the brick pattern admits of. If a still greater degree of enrichment or elaboration is desired, the pattern must be abandoned for the diaper (see Plate XII.), in which there is no limit to fancy or invention. In the brick pattern it is necessary to retain a large proportion of the ground of each division entirely free from ornament, and to so dispose the ornamentation that it may relieve the severe line-work without impairing its distinctness. In a diaper pattern, any freedom may be taken either with the general forms or the enrichment introduced in them; and the enrichment may wander from one division to another. (See No. 1, Plate XIV., and No. 1, Plate XXIII.)

It is unnecessary to minutely describe the present designs further than to point out the principles they illustrate. No. 1 shows how a natural flower, properly conventionalised, may be introduced with pleasing effect. The arrangement of the joint lines is here more complex than in any of the preceding examples. The central vertical line is detached from all the others; and is so placed, with relation to the ornament, as to apparently belong to it, adding to its length, and connecting it more intimately with the frame-work. No. 2 has its joint lines arranged in a similar manner to the preceding; but the ornament, in this case strictly conventional, springs from each side of the vertical lines, and leaves the centre of each oblong division unoccupied. No. 3 shows another method of treating the joint lines with an enrichment carried up between the vertical ones. The ornament is strictly conventional and is unsymmetrically disposed. No. 4 has triple horizontal and vertical joint lines; and the ornament is placed towards the lower part and one end of the oblong division to impart a quaintness and freedom to the design.

As all these patterns are too elaborate to be carried over large surfaces, borders or bands have been added, designed in keeping with their general ornamentation.

Plate V

1

2

3

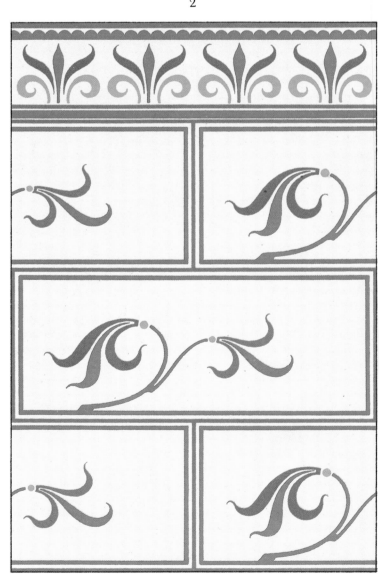

4

W & G AUDSLEY, INVEN. ET DEL.

Imp. Firmin-Didot & Cie, Paris

PLATE VI.

———————

In the previous Plates all the designs have been based on the brick pattern; we now come to those which illustrate widely different treatments. Nos. 1 and 2 show two varieties of the band treatment, in counter-changed colouring — the most satisfactory method of colouring which can be adopted in this style of wall pattern, as it helps to remove to a considerable degree the unavoidable hard effect of the banding. Analogous shades of one colour, such as are represented on the Plate, are much to be preferred to contrasting colours. When a very quiet result is aimed at, the counter-changed colours may be brought very close to each other in intensity; so close, indeed, as to blend together when viewed from a moderate distance. No. 1 shows the horizontal treatment with devices (dark on light and light on dark) placed in the centre of the bands. The devices thus disposed may consist of heraldic forms, symbols, monograms, or in fact any design the fancy of the artist may suggest. No. 2 shows the vertical treatment, with devices placed on the junctions of the light and dark bands, and accordingly rendered in counter-changed colours. Patterns produced on this principle are generally satisfactory, as they tend to distribute the colours, and break up the severity of the parallel lines. Of course the devices must be selected with reference to the possibility of their being divided up the centre and ren-dered in counter-changed colours, as is the fleur-de-lis in the present example.

Nos. 3 and 4 are the simplest forms of diaper-work, consisting of small flowers connected with or enclosed by diagonal lines. Patterns of this description are readily designed in almost endless variety. When executed in low-toned colours, they are very suitable for dados or the lower portions of walls; and, in a small scale, are appropriate decorations for the panels of screens, the backs of niches, recesses, &c.

Plate VI

2

4

1

3

W & G AUDSLEY, INVEN. ET DEL.

Imp. Firmin-Didot & Cie, Paris

PLATE VII.

DIAPER PATTERNS,

SUITABLE FOR WALL SPACES OF MODERATE DIMENSIONS.

———————

The four designs on this Plate are developed from the thirteenth century examples in the church of St. Mary, West Walton, Norfolk.*

Each design illustrates a different treatment of form and disposition of colour. No. 1 consists of circles containing devices, on a uniform ground of deep red, the spaces between the circles being relieved by small flowers. This pattern may have its colouring reversed, although the effect would hardly be so pleasing. No. 2 consists of squares placed on the angle, and alternating dark and light (like the squares of a chess-board), with counter-changed devices. The effect of this treatment is invariably good. The alternating squares may have the same device, simply counter-changed, as in No. 3. The chief difference between Nos. 2 and 3 lies in the arrangement of the dark and light squares. In the latter they do not alternate diagonally, but follow each other in diagonal bands; the effect is, accordingly, by no means so satisfactory as in the previous example. No. 4 is formed if circles of two colours, disposed in horizontal bands of light and dark grounds, the circles containing different devices in counter-changed colours. When used in the backs of arcades, or in any special wall spaces, this pattern is highly effective. Its pronounced character requires it, however, to be adopted with caution and judgment.

* These are illustrated in Colling's *Gothic Ornaments,* vol. I, pl. 62 and 63.

Plate VII

1

2

3

4

W & G AUDSLEY, INVEN. ET DEL.

Imp. Firmin-Didot & Cie, Paris

PLATES VIII AND IX.

BROCADE PATTERNS IN ONE COLOUR UPON A LIGHT GROUND,
SUITABLE FOR GENERAL WALL SURFACES.

———————

Brocade patterns, in the several treatments illustrated on these Plates, are appropriate decorations for walls where a medium degree of enrichment is desired. These patterns are very inexpensive, and are readily executed by simple stencilling. Any intensity can be secured by the use of contrasting or analogous tints; the former being illustrated on Plate VIII., the latter on Plate IX. In a colouring similar to Plate IX., brocade patterns form most agreeable and refined decorations for the panels and other surfaces of roofs and ceilings of considerable dimensions. These patterns do not admit of being cut up into small strips, their greatest charm existing in their flowing continuity.

In designing brocade patterns the artist must endeavour to keep the ornament and ground fairly balanced, and to distribute the ornament uniformly, so as to avoid a spotty effect. The ground spaces must not show more prominently in one part of the design than another. The designs given are properly treated in this respect.

The variety possible in brocade patterns is absolutely limitless, and there are no restrictions with reference to their colouring. When several colours are introduced on light grounds, they should not be rendered uniform, but rather be broken up or graduated in intensity, ever changing throughout the work. This produces a soft and artistic result, which never can be arrived at with absolutely uniform stencilling. For special and important works several shades or tones of each colour may be used and blended, according to pleasure, or as experience may dictate.

Plate VIII

1

2

3

4

W & G AUDSLEY, INVEN. ET DEL.

Imp. Firmin-Didot & Cie, Paris

Plate IX

W & G AUDSLEY, INVEN. ET DEL.

Imp. Firmin-Didot & Cie, Paris

2

1

PLATE X.

BROCADE PATTERNS IN GOLD UPON DARK GROUNDS.

These patterns are similar in all essential points to those just described; they are executed in gold upon dark colours for the purpose of showing the peculiarly rich yet quiet effect produced. To use these in gold for large surfaces would of course be very expensive, and the result would hardly be satisfactory. For the lower parts of chancel or sacrarium walls, the backs of blind-arcades, sedilia, niches, and similar positions, gold brocade patterns are most suitable.

These designs may be produced in harmonious tints, similar to those illustrated on the two preceding Plates.

Plate X

2

1

W & G AUDSLEY, INVEN. ET DEL.

Imp. Firmin-Didot & Cie, Paris

PLATE XI.

———<———

The twelve designs on this Plate illustrate the different styles of devices which may be adopted as powderings for walls or roofs. They comprise simple ornamental forms, heraldic devices, animals, birds, symbols, emblems, and monograms.

Powderings are appropriate enrichments for large surfaces of wall where a simple system of decoration is aimed at. They can be closely placed (as indicated on the Plate), or dispersed at considerable distances, and they may be applied in any mode of colouring. Where the walls are light and a very quiet effect is desired, they may be stencilled a few shades darker than the ground tint, as the patterns on Plate IX. Where a more decided effect is desired, the powderings may be in some rich contrasting colour. Such designs as Nos. 1, 2, 3, 10, 11, and 12 may be executed in two or more colours. Powderings may also be light upon dark grounds, as the small flowers of pattern No. 4 on Plate VI. When carried out in gold, as in the series here given, they are only appropriate for special purposes, such as dados of chancels, walls behind altars, backgrounds of niches, panels of screens, or pulpits. In domestic architecture, powderings may be carried over the entire walls of halls, staircases, or important apartments, above dados of woodwork or painting.

Powderings are very useful for the enrichment of spaces round medallions, canopies, &c., where other patterns would be liable to cause a confused effect : they are in their nature the most flexible of all modes of surface decoration.

Plate XI

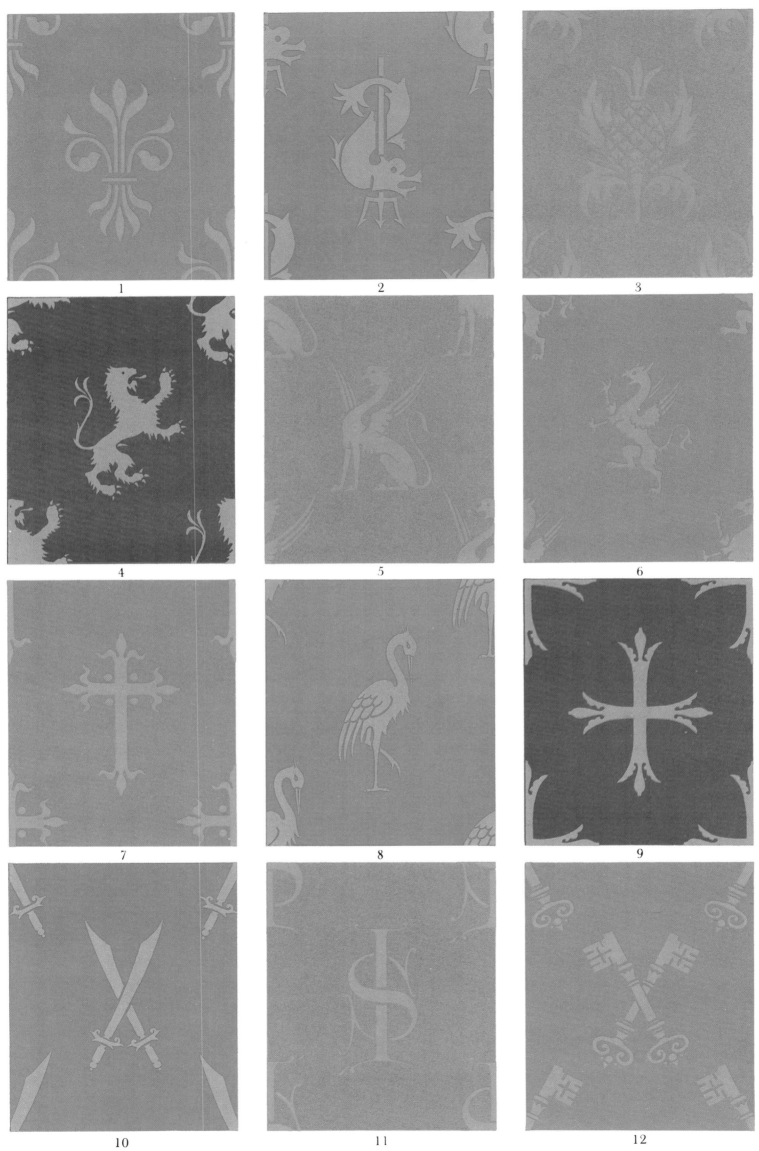

W & G AUDSLEY, INVEN. ET DEL.

Imp. Firmin-Didot & Cie, Paris

PLATE XII.

DIAPER PATTERNS IN RICH COLOURS ON LIGHT GROUNDS,
FOR WALL SPACES OF MODERATE DIMENSIONS.

The four patterns on this Plate illustrate different methods of diapering, suitable for wall spaces upon which a light and rich effect is desired. Nos. 1 and 3 are most suitable for spaces which are narrow and high, whilst Nos. 2 and 4 are more suitable for low and long spaces between horizontal lines. The latter patterns may also be used for the decoration of the shafts of circular pillars.

All the designs may be executed without gold, its place being taken by gold-colour or some other harmonious colour.

Four borders of suitable character are placed above the diapers.

Plate XII

1

2

3

4

W & G AUDSLEY, INVEN. ET DEL.

Imp. Firmin-Didot & Cie, Paris

PLATE XIII.

DIAPER PATTERNS IN GOLD ON RICH COLOURED GROUNDS, SUITABLE FOR THE LOWER PORTIONS OF WALLS.

This Plate shows four different diaper treatments, in gold and rich colours. These designs, as rendered, are, like those on Plate X., most suitable for small surfaces of wall, close to the eye, or which are required to be extremely rich in effect, *e. g.* the lower wall surfaces, backgrounds of tracery-work, and blind-arcades adjoining altars. They are also proper enrichments for the panels of screens, organ cases, &c.

Pattern No. 1 consists of counter-changed red and gold lozenges, divided by green bands dotted with gold. This design, and, indeed, all designs based on the same type, may be rendered in colours only, as the patterns on Plates VII. and XXII. The same remark applies to the other designs on the Plate under consideration. Pattern No. 2, formed of squares divided by interlacing bands, may be placed lozenge-wise if preferred. This design executed in simple colouring would form an appropriate ceiling decoration between timber beams or mouldings. Patterns Nos. 3 and 4 require no special comment.

Plate XIII

1

2

3

4

W & G AUDSLEY, INVEN. ET DEL.

Imp. Firmin-Didot & Cie, Paris

PLATE XIV.

DIAPER PATTERNS IN GOLD ON RICH COLOURED GROUNDS,
SUITABLE FOR THE LOWER PORTIONS OF WALLS.

The two patterns on this Plate, executed either in gold on deep-coloured grounds, as re-presented, or in colour upon colour, are suitable for dados or the lower portions of walls, where great richness of detail is desired. The diagonal and zig-zag treatments preclude their being adopted for large and elevated surfaces.

Both these patterns would be perfectly satisfactory in the colouring of Plate IX., the bands being tinted a little deeper than the general ground.

Plate XIV

2

1

W & G AUDSLEY, INVEN. ET DEL.

Imp. Firmin-Didot & Cie, Paris

PLATE XV.

DIAPER PATTERNS AND BORDERS IN RICH COLOURS UPON GOLD GROUNDS,
SUITABLE FOR SMALL WALL SPACES WHERE GREAT RICHNESS IS REQUIRED.

The five patterns on this page are after the style of the elaborate decorations of the Sainte-Chapelle, at Paris; but the colouring here adopted is not so bright as that followed by the French artists. This style of painting, in which all the colours are separated from the gold ground by black outlines, is of the most expensive description, and, on account of its intense richness, requires to be most sparingly used.

Pattern Nos. 4 shows how gold may be economised by the adoption of a coloured ground in designs of this style.

Patterns Nos. 1 and 2 are also suitable for the enrichment of the shafts of pillars of moderate dimensions, whilst Nos. 3, 4 and 5 may be used as bands for shafts in plain colours.

Plate XV

1

2

3

4

5

W & G AUDSLEY, INVEN. ET DEL.

Imp. Firmin-Didot & Cie, Paris

PLATE XVI.

BANDS AND BORDERS IN RICH COLOURS UPON LIGHT GROUNDS,
SUITABLE FOR DIVIDING WALL SURFACES.

The bands and borders on this Plate are suitable for the horizontal and occasionally for the vertical dividing of plain walls, or of those enriched with patterns similar to those of Nos. 1 and 2, Plate III.; Nos. 1 and 2, Plate IV.; Nos. 1, 2, 3, and 4, Plate V.; and Nos. 1, 2, 3, and 4, Plate XII.

All the designs may be executed upon the general ground tint of the wall, or upon a band of a deeper tint, as in band No. 7. On band No. 9 is shown a favourite method of introducing two ground tints. Bands Nos. 7 and 8 are designed after borders found in early illuminations; and No. 2 is suggested by a Romanesque painted band in the church of Tournus (Saône-et-Loire). Such bands as Nos. 3, 5, and 6 are suitable for decorations underneath the moulded wall plates or cornices of aisle or nave roofs.

Corner-pieces are given in four instances, to show the best method of uniting bands which meet together at right angles.

Plate XVI

W & G AUDSLEY, INVEN. ET DEL.

Imp. Firmin-Didot & Cie, Paris

PLATE XVII.

BANDS OF ELABORATE DESIGNS IN RICH COLOURS.

All the bands on these Plates are of the richest description commonly used for the decoration of walls in ecclesiastical and domestic buildings. They are suitable for all salient positions; and would prove highly effective above dados of plain rich colours, such as dark green deep red, slate-colour, brown, &c.; or spaces of wall covered with quiet patterns in deep colours, as Nos. 1, 2, and 4, Plate II.; Nos. 3 and 4, Plate III.; and Nos. 1, 2, and 4, Plate VI.

The five bands on Plate XVII. are developed from the ornamental portions of the twelfth century alphabet illustrated on Plates XXXIII. and XXXIV., and are accordingly highly appropriate for buildings in the Romanesque and Early Pointed styles. The gold, though very sparingly introduced, may be altogether omitted, and its tint imitated by a greenish or tawny yellow.

Plate XVII

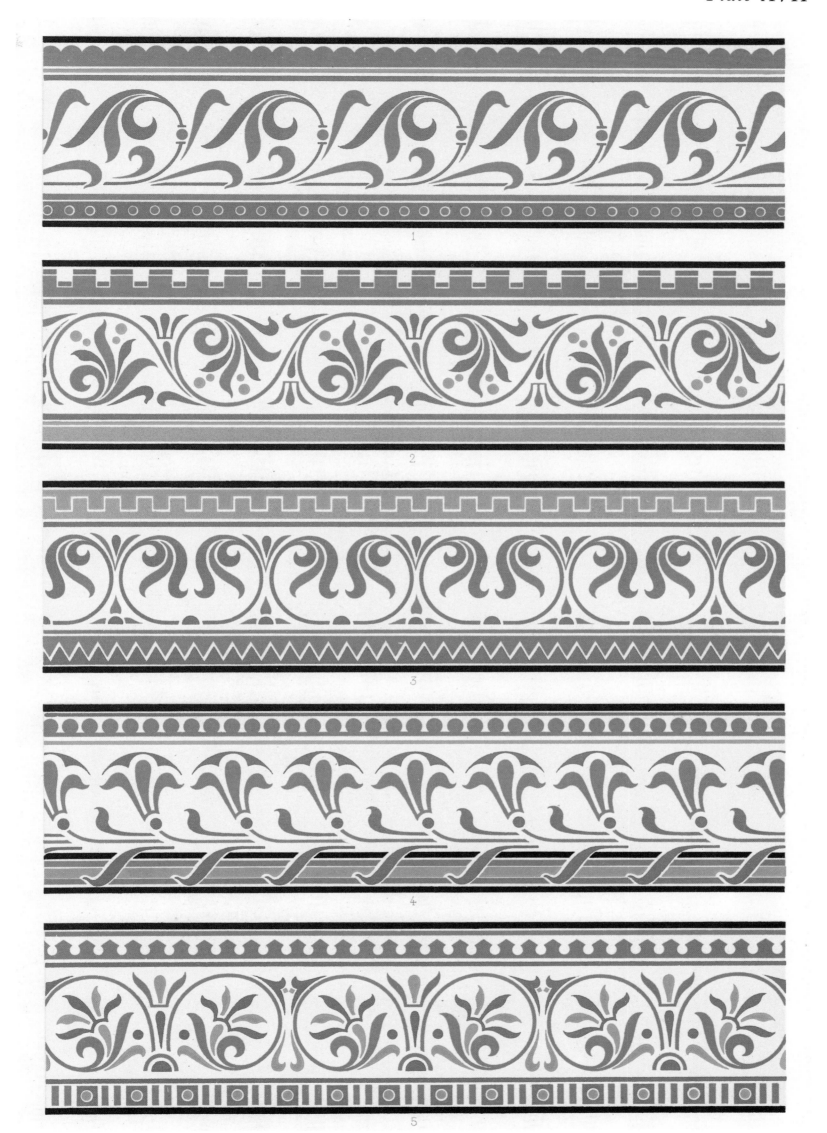

W & G AUDSLEY, INVEN. ET DEL.

Imp. Firmin-Didot & Cie, Paris

PLATE XVIII.

BANDS OF ELABORATE DESIGNS IN RICH COLOURS.

———————

The five bands on Plate XVIII. are expressive renderings, in flat colours, of the highly characteristic thirteenth century stone carvings of Laon cathedral. They are, therefore, appropriate for buildings in the Early English and Early Decorated styles, and the Early Pointed styles of France. The gold in these may be substituted by gold-colour.

Plate XVIII

W & G AUDSLEY, INVEN. ET DEL.

Imp. Firmin-Didot & Cie, Paris

PLATE XIX.

BANDS OF ELABORATE DESIGNS IN RICH COLOURS.

———————————

The five bands on Plate XIX. illustrate the chief modes in which animals, birds, and fishes are introduced in continuous narrow spaces. Bands Nos. 1, 2, and 3 are simply ornamental dispositions. No. 4 is symbolical, and forms an appropriate enrichment for the walls of a baptistery. No. 5 shows the manner in which the supporters of a shield may be introduced as ornamental features. These few examples will suggest to the decorative artist an endless number of simple combinations.

Plate XIV

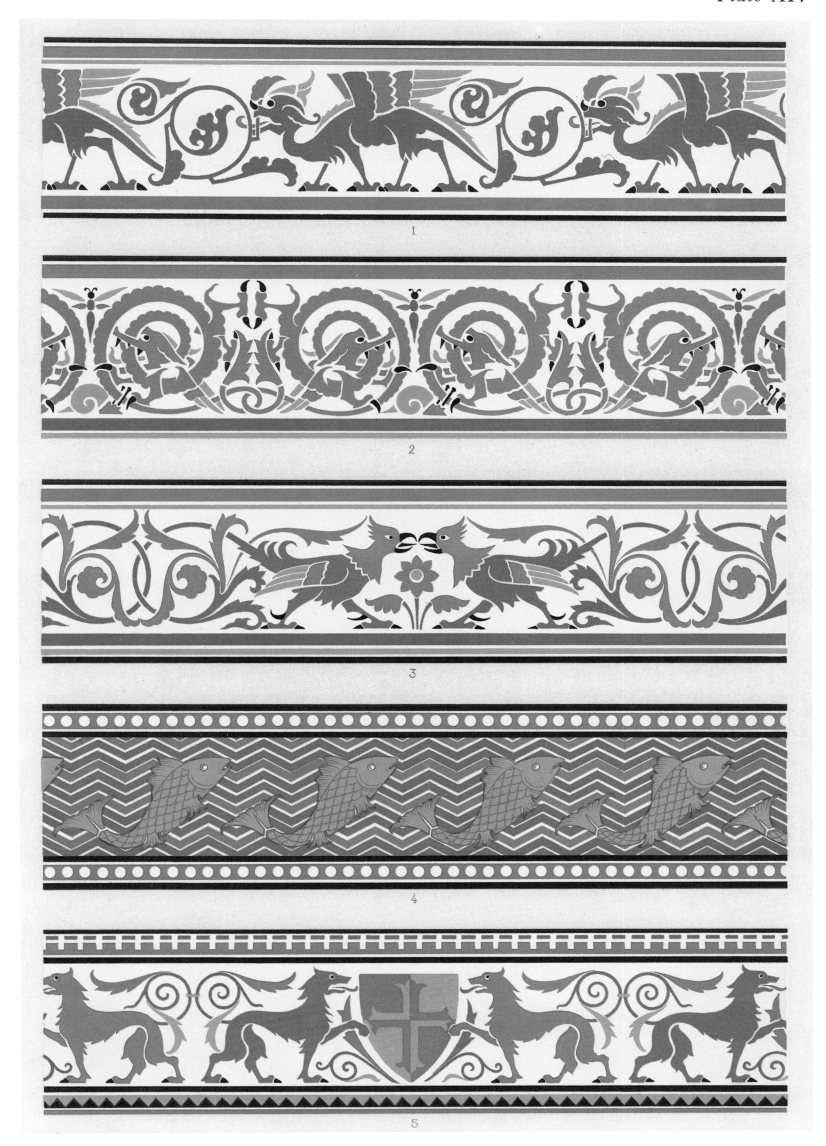

W & G AUDSLEY, INVEN. ET DEL.

Imp. Firmin-Didot & Cie, Paris

PLATE XX.

BATTLEMENTED CRESTINGS, FOR UPPER DIVISIONS OF DECORATED WALL SURFACES.

Battlemented crestings or cornice bands, such as are represented on this Plate, are suitable for the upper edge of decorated surfaces of walls above which there are plain tinted spaces. Where there are no structural cornices these crestings may be painted immediately under roofs or ceilings.

Crestings Nos. 1 and 2 are suitable for Early and Middle Pointed buildings; No. 3, for Late Pointed work; and Nos. 4 and 5 are of French character (thirteenth and fourteenth centuries).

Plate XXI

1

2

3

4

5

6

W & G AUDSLEY, INVEN. ET DEL.

Imp. Firmin-Didot & Cie, Paris

PLATE XXII.

DIAPER, SPIRAL, AND ZIG-ZAG PATTERNS FOR THE ORNAMENTATION OF PILLARS.

————◦———◦————

The nine patterns on this Plate are suitable for the enrichment of circular pillars, and illustrate the several methods which were very commonly adopted during the middle ages. All the patterns may be executed on dark grounds if preferred, and may be developed to any degree of richness. Patterns Nos. 2, 4, 5, and 6 may be entirely gold on rich green, red, or brown grounds; or, if the shafts are small, may be in black or dark green upon gold grounds. Black and gold always produce a rich and refined effect on small pillars, especially when the bases and capitals are gilded.

Plate XXII

1

2

3

4

5

6

7

8

9

W & G AUDSLEY, INVEN. ET DEL.

Imp. Firmin-Didot & Cie, Paris

PLATE XXIII.

PATTERNS IN RICH COLOURS UPON GOLD GROUNDS FOR PILLAR DECORATION.

———————◦—⟨—◦———◦————

The two patterns on this Plate represent the rich description of shaft decoration followed in the Sainte-Chapelle, at Paris. The colouring here is more subdued than in the French work. Ornamentation of this class has a very telling effect in arcades and sedilia, or indeed in any situations where the pillars are relieved by a harmonious background of colour.

These designs and others of the class form appropriate, though somewhat expensive, diapers for organ pipes.

Plate XXIII

W & G AUDSLEY, INVEN. ET DEL.

Imp. Firmin-Didot & Cie, Paris

1

2

PLATE XXIV.

PILLARS, ARCH-MOULDINGS, AND STRINGS CONVENTIONALLY RENDERED, FOR WALL DECORATION.

———·⟨·———

This Plate presents four arch-mouldings, four capitals, four bases, four plinths, and four strings, all conventionally rendered for flat painting, and capable of being produced by stencilling alone. In Nos. 1 and 2 the capitals are from circular examples, such as are met with in English Early Pointed work; Nos. 2 and 3 have capitals with square abaci, such as are commonly found in French architecture.

It will be observed that the several types of bases are here expressed by being rendered as it were in vertical section. The same remark applies to the abaci and neck-mouldings of the capitals. A study of this Plate will enable the artist to render with ease any style of capital or base which may take his fancy, or appear best suited for the work in hand.

Plate XXIV

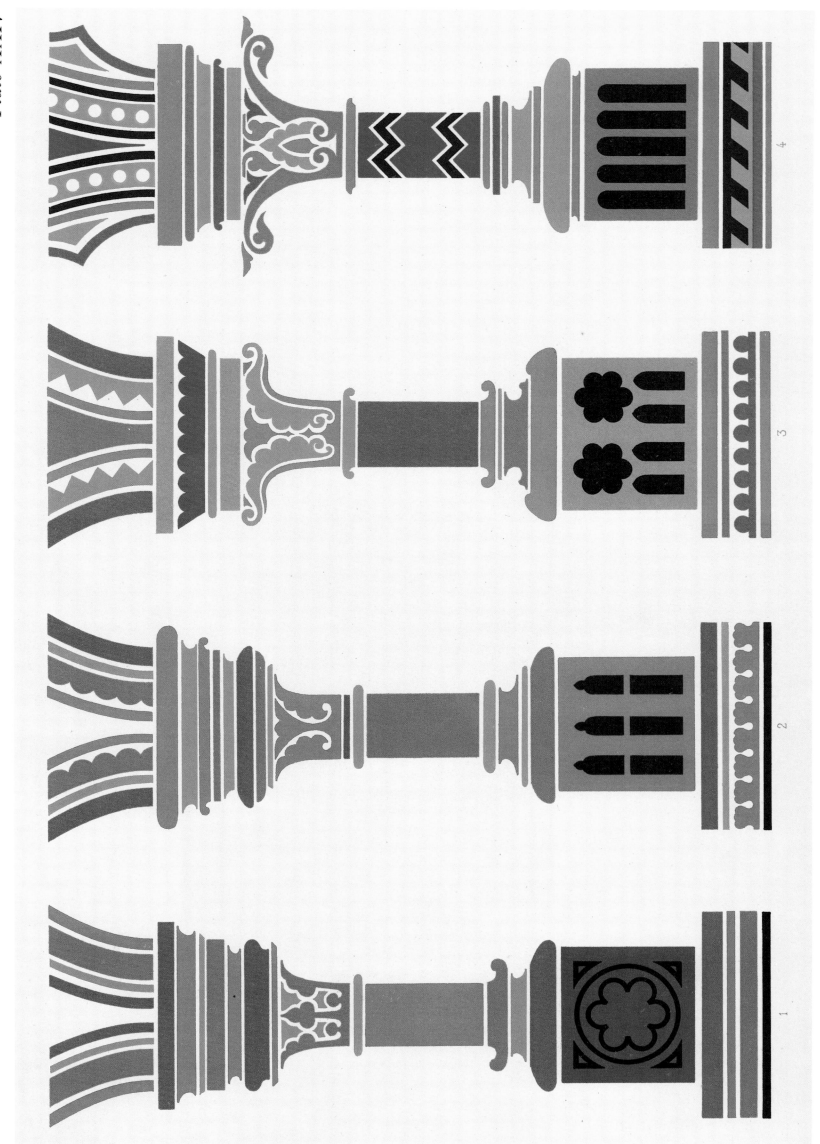

W & G AUDSLEY, INVEN. ET DEL.

Imp. Firmin-Didot & Cie, Paris

PLATE XXV.

COLONNADE AND ARCADES CONVENTIONALLY RENDERED,
FOR THE DECORATION OF WALLS.

———·o—<·—o———

The drawings on this Plate clearly show how colonnades and arcades may be represented with great effect upon flat walls, without in any way imitating similar features in construction. Arcades, such as Nos. 2 and 3, when executed on darker grounds, form most effective and appropriate dados under aisle windows, &c. When executed on a large scale, across blank walls, figures may appropriately be introduced between the pillars; or a hanging, conventionally treated, and covered with a brocade pattern, powdering, or diaper, may extend from capital to capital, filling the space downwards.

Plate XXV

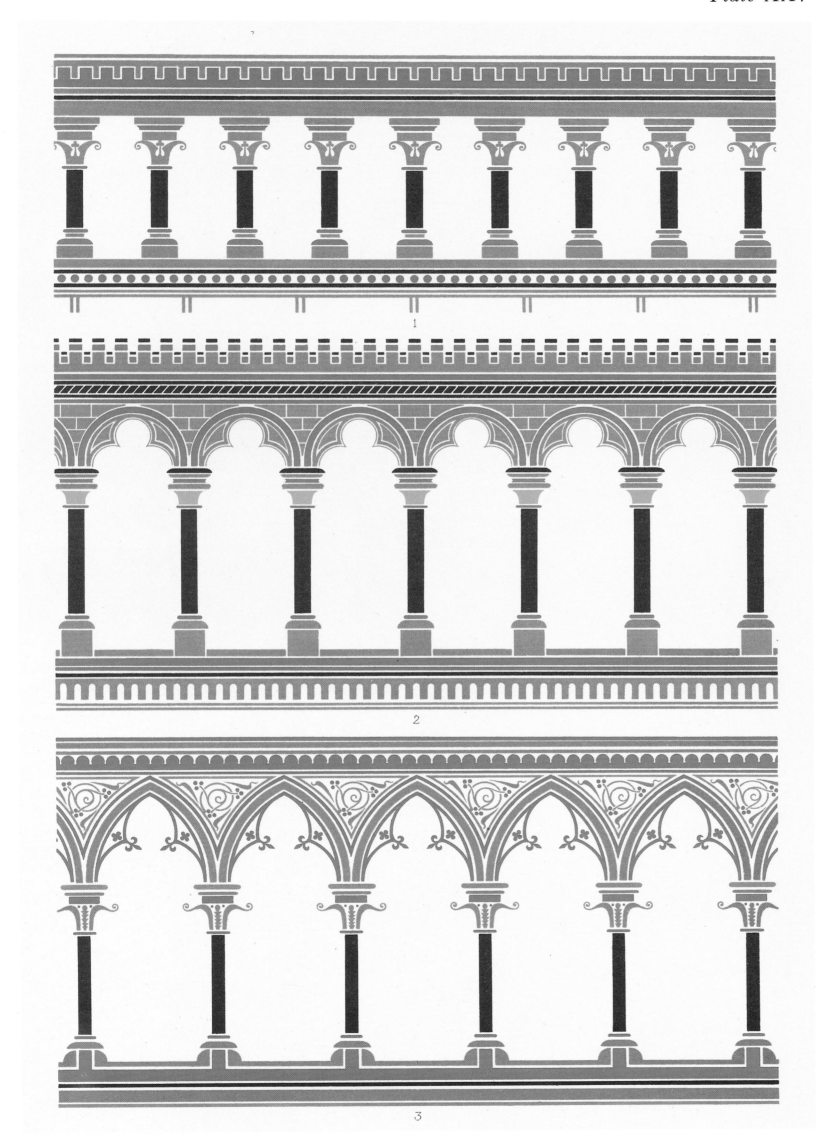

W & G AUDSLEY, INVEN. ET DEL.

Imp. Firmin-Didot & Cie, Paris

PLATES XXVI AND XXVII.

FINIALS, CROCKETS, AND MOULDINGS CONVENTIONALLY TREATED FOR THE DECORATIONS OF WALLS.

On these Plates is given a very complete series of designs, illustrating the most effective methods of rendering finials and crockets in flat painting.

On Plate XXVI. the designs are chiefly of an English character, although in crockets Nos. 3 and 4, a French feeling is evident.

On Plate XXVII. all the designs are of the French type.

The artist, with the other examples to guide him, will have no difficulty in forming finials to match the various crockets given on Plate XXVI., or in forming crockets from the finials on Plate XXVII.

All the designs in these Plates can be executed by stencilling.

Plate XXVI

W & G AUDSLEY, INVEN. ET DEL.

Imp. Firmin-Didot & Cie Paris

Plate XXVII

W & G AUDSLEY, INVEN. ET DEL.

Imp. Firmin-Didot & Cie Paris

PLATE XXVIII.

ANIMALS AND BIRDS CONVENTIONALLY RENDERED
FOR THE DECORATIONS OF WALLS.

The designs on this Plate show the modes of rendering animals and birds, in flat painting, in the chief positions and details in which they appear in mediæval architecture. These designs may be introduced in canopy-work painted over figure subjects, or in representations of architectural structures so frequently introduced in the figure subjects themselves. No. 9 is a rendering of one of the fine animals which are placed on the angles of the parapet round the towers of the cathedral of Notre-Dame, at Paris.*

All the designs are so carefully drawn with relation to the architectural features from which they spring, that a further description is quite unnecessary. They can all be executed by stencilling.

*A drawing of this animal, as it appears in sculpture, is given in the Authors' *Popular Dictionary of Architecture and the Allied Arts;* article *Animal*, vol. I, p. 142. From which the artist can realise how readily the character and spirit of sculptured works can be retained in such flat decorative painting as is represented on this Plate.

Plate XXVIII

W & G AUDSLEY, INVEN. ET DEL.

Imp. Firmin-Didot & Cie Paris

PLATE XXIX.

DECORATIONS FOR THE TIMBERS OF ROOFS AND CEILINGS.

———————⟨—◦—⟩———————

The seven designs on this Plate illustrate different methods of decorating the soffits of beams, purlins, and rafters employed in the construction of open timber roofs and ceilings. Although all the designs are shown upon coloured grounds, with slight modifications in treatment as regards colour, they may be applied direct to the wood itself, which, in most cases, forms an agreeable ground-work for coloured ornamentation. Black, blue, green, rich red, gold-colour, white, and gold, are effective upon oak, or any wood stained to resemble it in tint; all colours of a decidedly neutral character prove tame and ineffective. Beads or chamfers in gold or gold and black, as in Figs. 1 and 2, are always appropriate and telling in effect. Lines of bright or full-toned colours may be applied along the edges of square timbers to give clear definition to them, but they must be sparingly used in the decorative designs applied to their surfaces.

Plate XXIX

W & G AUDSLEY, INVEN. ET DEL.

Imp. Firmin - Didot & Cie Paris

PLATE XXX.

DESIGNS FOR THE SPACES BETWEEN THE RAFTERS OF TIMBER ROOFS.

In open timber roofs it is an almost invariable custom to show the under surfaces of the rafters, the spaces between them, when intended for decoration, being plastered. The four designs on this Plate illustrate effective methods of treating such narrow and elongated spaces, and also different modes of enriching the rafters when very elaborate results are aimed at. With simple designs in monochrome, as in Fig. 1, the natural wood of the rafters may be left untouched. The important consideration of expense in most instances prevents the rafters receiving anything beyond the simplest treatment.

In many cases the rafters, along with the spaces between them, are painted a uniform light tint, commonly vellum or some other tint slightly removed from white, and upon this coloured decorations are applied; the rafters being accentuated by a simple repeating pattern in strong neutral or low-toned colours. In roofs of large extent this is generally the most satisfactory method to adopt, especially in churches which are deficient of light.

Plate XXX

4

3

W & G AUDSLEY, INVEN. ET DEL.

Imp. Firmin-Didot & Cie Paris

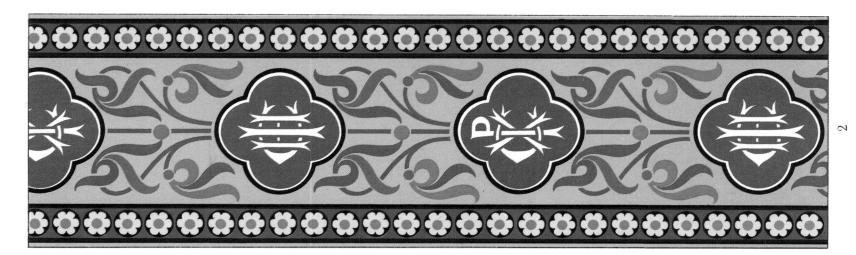

2

1

PLATE XXXI.

DESIGNS FOR THE SIDES OF THE ARCHED PIECES OF THE PRINCIPALS, &c.,
OF OPEN TIMBER ROOFS.

The eight designs on this Plate illustrate the several methods in which the sides of the curved or arched pieces, introduced in open timber roofs, may be appropriately decorated. In certain mediæval roofs the curved pieces are carved, and these carvings are painted, as in the fine roof of the nave of Knapton church, Norfolk.* In others they are plain and enriched with patterns in colour, as in the roof of the nave of Palgrave church, Suffolk.† The designs, Nos. 6, 7, and 8, are based on the patterns in the latter roof.

In roofs where the timbers are stained and varnished, or left in the natural wood, patterns such as Nos. 1, 5, 6, 7, and 8, stencilled on in some dark harmonious tint or black, have a pleasing effect. Nos. 2 and 3 are suggestions for rich floral and conventional scroll-work decorations.

* Illustrated in Brandon's *Open Timber Roofs of the Middle Ages*, pls. 36-38.
† *Ibid.*, pls. 21, 22.

Plate XXXI

W & G AUDSLEY, INVEN. ET DEL.

Imp. Firmin-Didot & Cie Paris

PLATE XXXII.

FOURTEENTH CENTURY ALPHABETS.

———◇———

The Alphabets given on this Plate, from a manuscript in the authors' possession, are peculiarly suitable for the inscriptions frequently introduced along with the ornamental decorations in buildings of the mediæval styles. The capital letters are of good form and full of spirit; and the text letters are uniform in treatment and very easily distinguished.

Plate XXXII

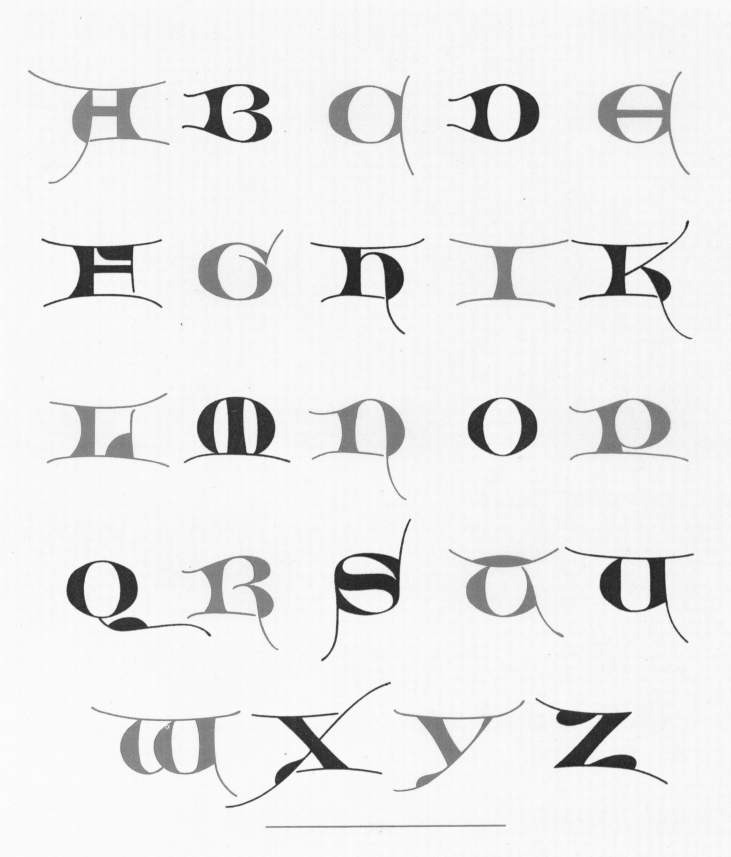

W & G AUDSLEY, INVEN. ET DEL.

Imp. Firmin-Didot & Cie Paris

PLATES XXXIII AND XXXIV.

TWELFTH CENTURY ALPHABET OF INITIAL LETTERS.

———————<————————

The beautiful alphabet given on these Plates is from a twelfth century manuscript, known as "Cardinal Mazarine's Bible," preserved in the National Library, at Paris. As a motive for most graceful and characteristic ornamentation, few, if any, mediæval alphabets exceed this. Every letter is perfect and truly beautiful in form, and is worthy of most careful study.

Plate XXXIII

W & G AUDSLEY, INVEN. ET DEL.

Imp. Firmin-Didot & Cie Paris

Plate XXXIV

W & G AUDSLEY, INVEN. ET DEL.

Imp. Firmin-Didot & Cie Paris

PLATE XXXV.

ALPHABET OF GOTHIC CHARACTER, SUITABLE FOR INSCRIPTIONS ON WALLS, &c.

The alphabet on this Plate has been developed from authorities of fourteenth century date, with the view of supplying a complete series of text letters of the simplest and most legible character, all unnecessary lines, flourishes, or other embellishments being omitted. The delicate line-work outside them and the ornamentation within the letters are quite matters of taste, and are not required for mural painting under any circumstances.

Plate XXXV

W & G AUDSLEY, INVEN. ET DEL.

Imp. Firmin-Didot & Cie Paris

PLATE XXXVI.

SPECIMENS OF FOURTEENTH AND FIFTEENTH CENTURY ILLUMINATED INITIALS.

———◇———

The six elaborate initials on this Plate are good examples of different schools of mediæval decoration. Nos. 1 and 2, are from an original early fifteenth century fragment in the possession of the authors. Nos. 3 and 4 are from fragments of the same date, preserved in South Kensington Museum. Nos. 5 and 6 are developed from fourteenth century examples in the possession of the authors.

Plate XXXVI

W & G AUDSLEY, INVEN. ET DEL.

Imp. Firmin-Didot & Cie Paris